PRAISE FOR PRACTICAL ADVICE FOR A BETTER WORLD

> "Mr. LeBoutillier delivers a collection of astute yet straightforward concepts supported by proficient and nonbiased arguments. A brilliant piece of work that politicians, bureaucrats, and decision-makers should read, highlight, and use as a blueprint to create a better world."
>
> ~Natacha Belair, Award-Winning Author of *A Stellar Purpose*

> "Ben LeBoutillier's thoughtful engagement in his debut work is well researched, carefully articulated, and well worth our own thoughtful engagement. Practical is in its title, and yet LeBoutillier presents us with a methodology that is as useful as it is helpful and inspiring. A better world is possible and within reach, especially with this gem in hand."
>
> ~Rev. Heather Wood Davis

" *Our country is at a crossroad. There has never been more division... So many conversations have to happen if we are to overcome the noise to seek actual societal solutions. Practical Advice for a Better World... is an ideal blueprint on how we could unite, proceed, and prosper. Kudos to Ben for a thoughtful, well-timed, and cogent book that far outreaches left vs. right arguments. Practical and refreshing!"*

~Ken Cavazzoni, Author of *Immortal*

" *I would invite every individual who cares about our shared life together to consider reading this thought-provoking and unifying book about important issues that we continue to discern in our world.*"

~Bradley Collins, MD, Anatomist, Podcast Host

" *Practical Advice for a Better World is exactly what our society needs. Ben gets to the core of big issues and offers practical, sensible solutions that are truly refreshing. This book should be taught at schools and placed in the hands of movers and shakers everywhere.*"

~Steve Wright, NFL Player, Author

" *All systems, material and social, change over time. Some changes are positive (i.e., improving the human condition) and some are negative. In this writing, LeBoutillier suggests that substantial change is currently necessary but change on the margins rarely has more than a short-term positive *impact on the systems(s) addressed, and [he] recommends a more analytical approach. . . . LeBoutillier's proposed typology is comprehensive and provides a basic structure to begin discussions. He posits solutions with which I and others may not agree in part or in whole but which provide a basis for initiating conversations, and it is by conversation, not argument or rant, that useful change may be generated."*

~John W. Bates, PhD

Practical Advice for a Better World:
Real solutions for society's biggest discords, concerns, and hopes for the future.

by Ben LeBoutillier

© Copyright 2024 Ben LeBoutillier

ISBN 979-8-88824-243-8

All rights reserved. No part of this publication may be reproduced, stored in a retrieval system, or transmitted in any form or by any means—electronic, mechanical, photocopy, recording, or any other—except for brief quotations in printed reviews, without the prior written permission of the author.

Published by

köehlerbooks™

3705 Shore Drive
Virginia Beach, VA 23455
800-435-4811
www.koehlerbooks.com

PRACTICAL ADVICE
FOR A
BETTER WORLD

REAL SOLUTIONS FOR SOCIETY'S BIGGEST DISCORDS,
CONCERNS, AND HOPES FOR THE FUTURE.

BEN LEBOUTILLIER

VIRGINIA BEACH
CAPE CHARLES

To my son and your generation,
that you may know a better world.

CONTENTS

Part 1: Exordium
To the Reader ... 3
Preface ... 5
Introduction ... 9
Low-Hanging Fruit ... 15

Part 2: Individual Concerns and Matters of the Citizenry
1. Pathways to Citizenship ... 20
2. Coming of Age ... 28
3. Marriage ... 42
4. Land Tenure ... 48
5. Consumer Rights ... 62
6. Healthcare ... 75

Part 3: Common Concerns and Matters of the Governmet
7. Elections and Psephology ... 92
8. Means of Governance ... 106
9. Taxation ... 126
10. Justice and Jurisprudence ... 143
11. Aid and Adminicle ... 157
12. States of Emergency ... 177

Part 4: Epilogue
Unification ... 188
Afterword ... 202

PART 1
EXORDIUM

TO THE READER

WITH SEVERAL MILLION titles published each year, why bother with this one? Why should you spend your time reading it, and why did I spend mine writing it?

This book is about you, me, and our world—the world we inhabit, love, hate, and wish to improve. The pages of this book are as advertised—practical advice for a better world. *Practical advice* because the ideas herein are tangible and doable; there are no rants, complaints, or soliloquies. *Better world* because that's the goal—to make the world better, for you, me, others, and those who come after us.

I am different from you, as are you from the next person, and that person from all others. Each has individual concerns and a unique vision for a better world. Nevertheless, what follows is universal. I have not outlined my own fantasy world or idealistic notions; rather, this work identifies and corrects society-wide systems that affect us all. Only after such societal infrastructure—as I've called it—is appropriately mended can the next phases begin.

Whether we wish to relax on a porch, start a business, feel financially secure, fix the climate, or see human beings on other planets, we currently labor in vain upon an unsteady foundation. That fractured concrete is exactly what this book addresses, rising to the occasion with real, practicable solutions that, once in place, will reveal untold possibilities.

Much of what we—as societies and as individuals—face every day is exceedingly complex, yet so much more doesn't have to be. The opportunities for efficiency and widespread appeal are nearly overwhelming. Few voices, it seems, have announced these possibilities; regrettably, those that have often ignore or underappreciate the aforementioned faulty foundation that must—indeed *must*—be addressed to allow for the changes needed before one can confidently relax on the porch, step foot on an alien world, or anything in between.

Blueprints abound. All around us are designs for mansions and townhouses and bungalows and off-the-grid vans and cabins and high-rises and more. Opposing opinions argue nonstop about which is better and for whom, or if a universal floor plan is sufficient. I don't want to make another blueprint because I see that there is a larger, more fundamental issue at hand. Instead, I want to point out that we need to grade the land and remove the shack currently thereon. Furthermore, I want to tell you how. Let's take care of that first; then, homes can be built.

With high hopes.

PREFACE

> *I must study politics and war that my sons may have liberty to study mathematics and philosophy. My sons ought to study mathematics and philosophy, geography, natural history, naval architecture, navigation, commerce, and agriculture, in order to give their children a right to study painting, poetry, music, architecture, statuary, tapestry, and porcelain.*
>
> ~John Adams

> *Let us fight for a new world—a decent world—that will give men a chance to work, that will give youth a future and old age a security.*
>
> ~Charlie Chaplin, from The Great Dictator

PRACTICAL ADVICE FOR a Better World is meant to uplift, unite, and inspire, but it was conceived in the tristful sentiments of disaffection, disillusion, division, and generalized despair. I was frustrated when voting for the first time. Given the seemingly countless people in the country, why was the highest office in the land a contest between two deplorables, neither of which had the decency nor respectability to lead a mule, let alone a country? I leaned conservatively in some areas, liberally in others, yet found more than anything that neither side's supposed solutions would improve anything.

I was baffled when the owner of a thriving local restaurant told me that the cost of employees' medical insurance prevented him from affording a full complement of staff. I was saddened when an industrious coworker told me that the government was several years delayed in processing citizenship applications; his would, almost certainly, not be addressed for more than a decade. I was troubled when a medical student told me that he was learning more about regulation and insurance than about healing the sick. I was demoralized when selling a handful of stocks subjected me to a hellish and horrendously complicated tax return; the paperwork was little worth the investment. I was heartbroken when I realized that policies designed to unite races and champion social equity almost always impeded those outcomes.

In a country—in a world—inhabited by so many intelligent, so many smart, assiduous, and capable people, how is there such widespread mismanagement? How does democracy become kakistocracy? Where are the sensible authorities?

Inappropriate constraints are the roots of our seeming inability to build a world equal to our potential. Instead of enjoying a comprehensive conversation about societal needs and how to fund them, we are constrained to bickering about whether tax rates should shrink or swell. Where is the discussion about the system of taxation itself? Amid the vast complexities of healthcare, we limit ourselves to asking how to mandate medical insurance. In the end, we constrain discussions, hamstring problem-solving, thwart collaborative creativity, and cavil about irrelevancies.

Notwithstanding, our biggest obstacle is, unfortunately, each other. The divisive dead ends to which our dialogues lead force us into camps that we don't even like. Then there we are, pitted against one another, demonizing those on the other side, and stubbornly refusing to identify common goals. As one person sits upon less insurance, and another upon more, aren't they—aren't we—*both* seeking a robust and fair medical system? If we begin at that common goal and expand our considerations outward, agreeing to consider—that is, to pause and hear—each other's opinions, we very likely will find an agreeable solution. Ironically enough, that resolution will, almost certainly, be altogether outside of the camps we started in.

∽

The goal of this book is to present ideas around which we can all unite. In public arenas of discussion, there are strong divisions growing more entrenched. Calls for unity, unfortunately—despite their purported goals—often do little more than cast certain groups in the right and others in the wrong. No real unification is attempted. I used to expend much mental energy blaming those of opposite views for the world's problems (and they probably thought the same of me), but one day I decided to think of them as people. I realized that we often share common goals but that our approaches had been so limited that we were incapable of finding acceptable solutions around which to rally. Political jousting has ruined our ability—and our desire—to cooperate.

Prior to an election, I would take a survey to discover the candidates with whom I most aligned, but the questions were hardly helpful. They were always binary yes/no—do you support *A* or *B*—questions because that was all the candidates represented. What about when the answer is neither *yes* or *no*, *A* or *B*, but something altogether different? It's not about blanket amnesty nor mass deportation, for neither is a panacea. Rather, why are the pathways to citizenship so confounded that they are altogether avoided? And what's the point of laws that cannot reconcile justice?

In this book, dear reader, you will find an altogether different discussion. The topics are familiar, but the dialogues are new. Because the conversations have led us astray and distracted us from worthwhile solutions, let us, in these pages, abandon that approach and consider a colloquy of new strategies, new visions, new cooperation. But more than philosophy, we need solutions. We need actionable, acceptable resolutions that will elevate both spirit and society. We need practical advice for a better world. I offer it to you with high hopes and lofty expectations.

INTRODUCTION

> *We all want progress. But progress means getting nearer to the place where you want to be. And if you have taken a wrong turning, then to go forward does not get you any nearer. If you are on the wrong road, progress means doing an about-turn and walking back to the right road; and in that case the man who turns back soonest is the most progressive man. We have all seen this when doing arithmetic. When I have started a sum the wrong way, the sooner I admit this and go back and start over again, the faster I shall get on. There is nothing progressive about being pigheaded and refusing to admit a mistake. And I think if you look at the present state of the world, it is pretty plain that humanity has been making some big mistake. We are on the wrong road. And if that is so, we must go back. Going back is the quickest way on.*
>
> ~C.S. Lewis, from *Mere Christianity*

> *As American as anything about this thoroughly American new president was his fundamental faith that most problems came down to misunderstandings between people, and that even the most complicated problems weren't really as complicated as they were made out to be once everybody got to know one another.*
>
> ~David McCullough, from *Truman*

DREAMS RARELY DIE on their own; instead, they are killed. The culprit is a system of insensate injunctions.

The death of a dream is as universal as having a dream itself, and every person from every conceivable facet of life has had a dream—not merely a dry sweven or selfish longing, but at least one truly great dream that engulfed one's passions and kept the dreamer awake at night. What was it? The specific was as unique as each individual, but the theme was unvaried—sharing a passion that betters individual lives, builds communities, and improves the world.

In all but a few exceptional people, dreams die. While some were sickly or otherwise unable to mature, most dreams never had a chance. They were murdered. They were cut down in their prime. Was the killer the cold nature of reality? Life's vagaries and vicissitudes? Or perhaps the incontrovertible truths of necessity, scarcity, and inequality? None of these. The leading cause of death for hopes and dreams is harebrained regulation—misconceived, misguided, ill-begotten ordinances.

Life is hardscrabble enough, but we understand its realities, and do not fault it. Despairingly, though, even when the fog lifts enough that we can catch a glimpse of the Happy Isles, some ascendancy rises to shield it from view and muddy the path that leads there. After this has happened enough, we erroneously begin to view the ascendancies and their wretched veils as facts of life no different than the downward pull of gravity. While we must make peace with laws of nature, we need not and should not, however, content ourselves with foolish diktats or the people who promulgate them.

This book is for all people, from any land or custom, of any age or disposition. Although particularly designed for hapless Americans of the current era, it more broadly speaks to any place and any time. We all share a special few universal experiences that transcend time and space. From our forebearers several millennia ago, to our descendants several millennia hence, and beyond, most have had or will have a dream to make a more wholesome world, a more sensible world, a more just world . . . a better world. But very nearly always, that dream is killed by witless regulation.

We must excise, deracinate, and utterly dismantle unsensible red tape before we can even begin to debate the many controversies that politicians and powerbrokers use to divide us. They and other talking heads create clashing factions, but we must strive to unite rather than divide. There are many differences between people, yet all have had dreams to make the world a better place. Whether in small or big ways, everyone has felt that desire. Unfortunately, we are not at a place where we can share our dreams, debate their merits, and work toward the best ones. We are stuck in systems that smother dreams in their infancy. Therefore, let us unite around the idea of keeping dreams alive.

∼

Before proceeding with a more thorough investigation, we must establish several lemmata central to the reasoning found herein.

Lemma 1: Dreams

This book proffers a universal human desire to improve something. Some people have smaller ambits, like their household or family; others dream of reshaping the world. Sadly, though, the single biggest obstacle to effectuating those dreams is gormless regulation.

Please note two things:

1. The hindrance is not regulation, but *needless* regulation. This book is not a call for anarchy, not even for libertarianism. It is a call to remove the waste that weighs us down. Both advocates for big government *and*

champions of small government should be able to unite around the causes herein.

2. All dreams are important, but not all are grand. Most dreams are simple and wholesome; they are things like starting small businesses, sharing knowledge, and supporting causes. Of course, there are bigger dreams, too, like ending privation, realizing justice for all people, and establishing equilibrium with our planet's resources. Whether big or small, self-seeking or magnanimous, dreams are thwarted by inane precepts.

Lemma 2: Incentives

There are, broadly, two flavors of incentives—positive and negative; that is, reward and punishment. In the analogy of the carrot and the stick, the carrot is positive, and the stick negative. When people undertake their various purposes, they are encouraged by positive incentives and discouraged by negative ones.

A person's innate drive is strong, especially for the types of dreams upon which this book is based. Positive incentives do not need to be added nearly as much as negative ones need to be removed. Furthermore, a lack of positive incentives will not kill a dream that was poised to live, but a surfeit of negative incentives will almost certainly destroy it.

To offer a vignette for understanding: Suppose that a bread lover decides to open an artisan bakery. The internal motivation is to spend his days baking and selling healthy loaves to his community. This is his vision of bettering the world; it is his dream, and he has an internal drive to do it.

Positive incentives such as better income, self-employment, and designing his bakery are just the icing on the cake—salt on the crust, if you will. Chances are, though, that he would still attempt to make that dream a reality even if it meant earning less, taking on a business partner, and using a repurposed kitchen.

Negative incentives are licenses, fees, taxes, audits, and a bevy of legal hassles. He seeks to achieve his dream *despite* these dicta. Given enough of them, his dream will die. It will not die from within, but due to the system without.

When someone has a stay-awake-at-night dream, positive incentives are not necessary because the internal motivation is so incredibly powerful. However, negative incentives can, and often will, kill it. Therefore, positive incentives do not need to be applied; simply, negative ones need to be removed.

Lemma 3: Government

Whether for, against, or indifferent toward government, it is manifestly the most abundant source of regulation and the most authoritative enforcer of it. Since its influence is vast, penetrant, and unyielding, it must be treated with great scrutiny. The fundamental purpose of government is to stabilize society. Though the means and scope are subject to preference and philosophy, the following assertions are veracious:

First, majority opinions are not necessarily wise, neither are they necessarily righteous. Oppression is never far from absolute majority rule. Safeguards such as checks and balances are crucial for wholesome governance. Second, local regulations are easier to influence than international ones. As legislation moves toward larger ambits—state, federal, then global—individual voters lose their ability to meaningfully engage. Broad-scope legislation should be approached with reservation and caution.

Lemma 4: Anachronisms

Anachronism is something that belongs to another time. Outdated systems are inapposite impediments that bog progress and suffocate dreams. This doesn't mean that all past wisdom is now irrelevant. New paint, however, is seldom applied effectively unless the existing coat has been scraped away. The suggestions herein will be difficult to envisage unless the reader is willing to reimagine what currently exists and reinvent its descriptions.

Lemma 5: Citizenship and residency

Many people can physically be in the same country yet not share the same status. Though there are potentially many nuanced categories of citizenship and residency, these four are sufficient for the upcoming chapters:

1. Citizens are full-fledged members of the country who enjoy all the privileges and protections that it offers, such as voting and accessing benefits.

2. Non-citizen residents are long-term visitors, such as visaed workers and students, who are legally allowed to be in the country for extended periods of time. Though frequently on the pathway to citizenship, they are, nevertheless, not (yet) members of the citizenry and therefore lack its prerogatives.

3. Visitors are tourists, vacationers, and others who visit the country without expectations of attaining citizenship or staying long.

4. Illegal visitors have bypassed proper channels when entering the country. While some have entered accidentally or plan to stay only days, others have deliberately sidestepped the country's laws and plan to stay indefinitely.

LOW-HANGING FRUIT

> *The smell of the sweat is not sweet, but the fruit of the sweat is very sweet.*
>
> ~Amit Kalantri, from *Wealth of Words*

> *Why not go out on a limb? Isn't that where the fruit is?*
>
> ~Frank Scully, from *Scully's Scrapbook*

Daylight savings

Low-hanging fruit is easy to reach and can be obtained without great struggle. Abolishing Daylight Savings Time (DST) is this book's first piece of practical advice for a better world. This fruit is hanging so low that it's practically in the basket.

From its inception, the claim that DST lessens energy consumption has been easily dismissed. Furthermore, since its debut in World War I, energy usage across the planet has become unrecognizable to what it was in 1916. If DST ever *did* have a claim to reducing energy consumption, those days are long gone.

Not only is DST *not* considered a positive for society, it has skipped neutral and become a negative. Twice a year, every timekeeping or time-sensitive process must be adjusted. Minor inconveniences such as resetting several clocks are givens, but there are serious implications also. Medical records must be reconciled, often manually; international communication must be adjusted because not all countries use DST, and those that do enter and exit on different dates; and caregivers across the nation must prepare for a sudden surge of cardiovascular events that will be precipitated by DST's concomitant stress.

DST is an anachronism that is somewhere between annoying and harmful. The experiment has failed, and its lingering has become clutter. The easiest way to streamline a civilization and demonstrate willingness to make positive changes is to end DST once and for all. At the next changing of the clocks, split the difference, shift them by one-half-hour only, and let that be the end of it.

Sunshine laws

Supposedly, elected officials work for the people; if that's the case, then why is it so difficult to find their work record? Of most candidates on a ballot, the only easily obtained information is about making campaign donations. Where are the voting records of legislators, or the verdicts of courtroom judges? Technically, they are public record, and some may even exist within the deep recesses of the internet. Nevertheless, they are, for all intents and purposes, unobtainable by the average voter.

Sunshine laws are an attempt at government transparency. They require that governmental proceedings be publicly available. However, since *available* is not the same as *accessible*, we should stress the latter. Quarterly, all proceedings—especially legislation—should be organized and published as an easy-to-read compendium that is obtainable—free of charge—in person, by mail, or from the relevant agency's website, preferably downloadable within one click of the homepage.

Sunset laws

The existence of absurdly irrelevant statutes evinces lazy and inappropriate legislative management. Blue laws are the most obvious. They forbid certain activities on Sunday, commonly the sale of alcohol, tobacco, or both. Though many such laws are laughable or more inconvenient than deleterious, they reveal that good government intendance is severely lacking.

More insidiously, though, is the ignominious practice of enacting laws and never again reevaluating them. Historic laws are not, by nature, faulty, as large portions of Hammurabi's Code (c. 1750 B.C.) and Moses's Torah (c. 1400 B.C.) are still pertinent today. On the other hand, they contain many decrees that are simply outdated. All systems—not just lawmaking—require inspection and maintenance, yet the American corpus of law has seldom been subjected to reassessment, save for the one in a myriad that claws its way before the US Supreme Court. Lawmakers add and add, but never subtract. We would do well to split the ranks of lawmakers into two groups, assigning half to law making and half to law abrogating.

A more realizable approach, however, and the one offered herein, is to establish all new laws as sunset laws with expiration dates. When a sunset law is ratified, it is automatically scheduled for removal at a designated time. Sunset laws can persist, but they must be *re-ratified*; if they are not, then they are repealed. If laws are created this way, then they can never become vexatious clutter of a bygone era. Expirations of less than five years from ratification are recommended.

PART 2

INDIVIDUAL CONCERNS AND MATTERS OF THE CITIZENRY

CHAPTER 1

PATHWAYS TO CITIZENSHIP

> *The first requisite of a good citizen in this Republic of ours is that he shall be able and willing to pull his weight—that he shall not be a mere passenger.*
>
> ~Theodore Roosevelt

> *One law and one custom shall be for you and for the stranger who dwells with you.*
>
> ~Numbers 15:16 (New King James Version)

Types of residents

Before embarking on a proper discussion of pathways to citizenship, the differences between visitors, citizens, etc., must be clarified. The Introduction's note on citizenship and residency treated this point briefly, but to reiterate, the congeries of statuses applied to persons standing on a given country's soil can be consolidated into four broad categories: citizen, legal resident, visitor, and illegal.

Addressing the last first, regardless of the noun used—immigrant, alien, resident—a person here illegally has entered the country through means other than government-sanctioned channels and, definitionally, has no legal standing in the country, neither as a citizen nor guest.

Visitors are foreigners who enter the country legally without expectations of employment, lengthy stays, or attaining citizenship. Families on holiday, vacationers, and those on business trips fall into this category; they have plans neither to tarry nor plant roots.

Legal residents are students on visas, sponsored employees, asylum seekers, and other long-term residents who are, nevertheless, not citizens. Many in this category are actively working toward citizenship, yet many are not, as large numbers of legal residents, especially students, might plan to return to their countries of origin. For those who aspire toward citizenship, legal residency is the pathway thither. Even still, until attaining that goal, legal residents have no claims to the prerogatives of citizenship.

Citizenship is qualified by full-fledged membership in the country. Citizens, either from birth or through the immigration process, are afforded all constituent and concomitant privileges of citizenship, the most salient of which are voting and receiving aid from the government.

It is worth further noting that the category to which one belongs has no reflection on his or her character or worth. A citizen can be just as deplorable as an undocumented immigrant can be upstanding. The nation, however, must look to its citizenry and country the way that good parents look to their families and houses.

Illegal people have entered the house without invitation or notice. Perhaps they came with good intentions, perhaps they did not know where to knock and came around the back fence, but there is also a chance that they have come as thieves, or worse.

Visitors are dinner guests. Their presence is welcomed, but they were not invited to spend the week.

Legal residents are second cousins who come to spend the summer. They are quartered in the guest room and allowed to put their personal touch to it. They help with the dishes and cover their fair share of the grocery bills; notwithstanding, they are not members of the household. They do not get to excessively rearrange the furniture to accommodate their preferences. The house is not theirs to influence; in the same vein, leaky ceilings and moribund appliances are not their burdens to bear.

Citizens are the family, and the nation is their house. Each member of the family is mutually obliged to care for the house, guard it from malefactors, and see to its prosperity. As they are the ones who live there, they determine its fate.

The final point that needs consideration, or rather reiteration, is that the pathway to citizenship is through legal, long-term residency. It is the bridge between foreigner and citizen. Even though some non-citizens might spend many months or longer in the country, until they become citizens, there is a marked distinction between the two. Such is only appropriate, as the government's first duty it toward its citizens—those who are vested in the country, contributory thereto, and inextricably bound to its fate.

Sovereignty

No nation should feel guilted by the proposition of its own sovereignty. No scruple, compunction, or obloquy can avert the verity that every nation is its own master. While international cooperation is often to a nation's benefit, it remains incontrovertibly sovereign. As such, each nation has the privilege of determining its visitors, residents, and—indeed—its citizens.

The United States has a rich history of immigration. Its eclectic citizenry is united neither by race nor origin, but by values, uniquely American values that draw people from around the world—liberty, industry, enterprise, moxie, and others. To those who share such principles, the United States should—with judiciousness—be welcoming, but to those who abhor them, the United States should be wary and—if warranted—rejective.

Under the current system, immigration and the pathways to citizenship are egregious and unjust. Journeying through the process *honestly* is lengthy, convoluted, and expensive. Exploiting loopholes is far easier. There is also the alternative of living in the country under the guise of legality, enjoying its privileges and protections, while actually being illegal and guilty of affronting the nation's immigration laws, even if those laws are impractical or otherwise nonsensical.

The current system has made legal immigration and attainment of citizenship so slow and difficult that many long-time residents and valued members of communities are tragically illicit. They are American in spirit, values, and locale, but not in documentation. The failings of the current system have pushed many citizens who sympathize with their illegal counterparts to circumvent immigration altogether and make misguided proclamations that citizenship and non-citizenship should have no distinctions, that the United States should turn a blind eye to its borders or dismiss borders altogether, that no crime can be severe enough to warrant deportation, and more.

These are the wrong paths to tread. Citizenship is qualified by prerogatives denied to non-citizens, borders are important safety measures, and foreigners who reveal themselves as deplorables have overstayed their welcomes and relinquished their privileges of visitation. The appropriate solution lies in abolishing the broken ways of the current system and installing a new one that welcomes wholesome people, rejects those who are execrable, and does so in a timely manner.

Acceptance of new citizens

Because a nation is shaped by its citizenry, it should extend the privilege of citizenship with cautious circumspection. Accordingly, the United States should guard citizenship carefully and refuse to extend it for trifling and senseless reasons. For example, granting citizenship to anyone born on US soil, regardless of circumstance, is an abhorrent affront to the country's own sovereignty, good sense, and duty to act justly toward its current citizenry.

But this is not to suggest that the US should become ungenerous in welcoming new citizens nor forget that its foundations—and indeed every step of the construction—have been laid by those whose ancestors, not many generations ago, lived in other countries. Rather, the US must balance generosity to the immigrant with right action toward its own. Since the current policies accomplish neither of these, we must alter the approach drastically, remembering that the appropriate course of action is not to abolish distinctions between citizens and non-citizens, nor to desultorily extend citizenship to all, but to create a functioning system in keeping with the country's values.

For such a system, the following minimum attributes are proposed:

1. At birth, citizenship be granted only to individuals who are born to at least one citizen.

2. Between birth and childhood, citizenship be granted if the child's legal guardians are citizens, such as when parents who were not citizens at the time of the child's birth have attained citizenship, or the child has been adopted by citizens.

3. From adolescence onward, citizenship be granted only to applicants who have lived in the country several years and are law-abiding, debt-free, self-supporting, proficient in the country's language and history, and recommended by several citizens.

A note on amnesty

Amnesty, in this context, is the proposition that all undocumented immigrants currently living in the US be granted citizenship and pardons from any crimes associated with having resided in the country illegally. Some proponents of amnesty support it because of genuine desires to allow upstanding, but undocumented, members of the community to *come out of hiding* and officially join the US that they have called home for so long anyway. Some support amnesty because they feel that it's easier than remedying the current fractured system. Those people might be correct, but the purported *solution* will undeniably create even worse problems than we currently have. Still others champion amnesty for nefarious purposes, usually political ones.

In all cases, whether motivated by vice or virtue, the approach is misguided. Amnesty is a fleeting, miscalculated attempt at justice under an unjust system. While it might be kind to grant citizenship to honest, American-spirited illegals, it is equally unjust to the current citizenry to swell its ranks so suddenly. And yet the real danger lies not in the execution of such an order, but in the aftermath. Amnesty sets the precedents that broken systems should be circumvented rather than fixed, and that attempting to abide by the system or play by the rules is not as expedient as breaking those rules. The second, especially, rewards those who have broken the law and punishes those who have tried to follow it.

The most salutary way to welcome the long-term undocumented members of our communities into the citizenry while still acting justly toward current citizens—and those on the legal tract—while still maintaining the country's respectability and sovereignty, is to implement the aforementioned proposal of minimum attributes but with two modifications: First, grant pardons for the crime of having entered into and resided in the country illegally. Second, allow illicit tenure to qualify—to some degree—as time lived in the country.

But whether this form of *amnesty* is employed or not, a necessary follow-up *must* occur. The United States needs to be firm in the application of its policy henceforth. With quick, fair treatments of immigration and applications for citizenship, people won't feel the need to bypass the system. Consequently, those who do will have no claim to clemency. The US has hitherto been made a pushover and a chump by its policies. It needs to correct its disastrously ineffective system, create a new one, and then apply it.

~

While the guidance just set forth is, of course, non-exhaustive, and while all procedures are subject to exception for extraordinary circumstances, it is worth mentioning the distinct absence of certain allowances. Some special situations may provide cause for waiving the requirements of citizenship, but some others do not. Two circumstances that ought *not* receive special consideration when applying for citizenship are *asylum seekers*, and *relatives of citizens*.

Asylum seekers, such as refugees, flee oppressive or unstable countries and need new places to go. When the US wishes to shelter asylum seekers, only *entry* needs to be granted—not citizenship. The United States should always consider the pleas of desperate people and, with reasonable prudence, grant refuge into the country that considers itself such. But in these cases, *visas*—that is, approval of long-term legal residency—need expediting, not applications for citizenship. As to the second case—relatives of citizens—it is very similar to that of asylum seekers. Perhaps a visa should be issued in a timelier manner than usual, but as for gaining citizenship, there is no justifiable reason to expedite that process.

That said, when it comes to visas and other types of long-term visitation, these processes, too, must not be so inefficient and confusing as to provoke their avoidance. The processes need to be refactored and made effective and practicable. Until visas are solved, the pathway to citizenship cannot be. Their solutions are both alike and intertwined.

CHAPTER 2
COMING OF AGE

> *When I was a child, I spoke like a child, I thought like a child, I reasoned like a child. When I became a man, I gave up childish ways.*
>
> ~1 Corinthians 13:11 (English Standard Version)

> *Children are more than we think they are. They can do more than we think they can do. All they need is a vote of confidence from grownups, whom they will ultimately replace anyway. Their dream today will become the realities of tomorrow.*
>
> ~Wess Stafford, from *Too Small to Ignore*

Two ontogenetic divisions

At the outset of this book, I spoke briefly about anachronisms and how some notions or beliefs of a previous era persist. It is easy to envision how society can be hampered by maintaining outdated modes. Take, for example, communication. How much of our current circumstances would not exist if we insisted that letters in envelopes were the only reasonable form of long-distance correspondence? Or more to the point, what if we insisted that physicians and patients should be the only divisions of healthcare? We would deny ourselves the vital roles of nurses, mid-level practitioners, respiratory therapists, technicians, and so many more.

Since time immemorial, people have been separated into two categories—*youths* and *adults*—generally with some formal rite of passage between the two around the age of puberty. In our modern world, we have discarded the rites of passage and increased the age, but we have anachronistically kept the two categories.

The progression between youth and adult is long and drawn out, with responsibilities and privileges being incrementally added throughout the full decade between years fifteen and twenty-five, and well beyond that. Consider how seventeen-year-olds are admitted to pediatric wards despite having been medical-adults for many years. Eighteen-year-olds are privileged to vote and are legally responsible for themselves yet not—supposedly—responsible enough to consume alcohol. Adults at the threshold of their thirties can still be covered by their parents' health insurance.

Shortcomings of the current system

The ontogeny of a human—that is, its development—can be divided into as many stages as there are days in a lifetime. But still, there needs to be some arrangement of useful categories. Infants are obviously not fit to be the masters of their own lives nor participate in sacred civil duties; likewise middle agers have no need of parental consent before entering into binding agreements.

Under the current system, this arbitrary division between youth and adult is based upon age, set at the eighteenth year, but—not stopping there—the system has blurred the division and spread it out five or more years to either side, thereby creating a decade-long nebulous transition that renders the original demarcation—eighteen years—quite anticlimactic. A young person has more cause for celebration upon obtaining a driver's license or ordering a beer at a restaurant than he or she has at turning eighteen. The former two are informal yet distinct rites of passage in our society;

the latter is just another incremental step along the journey, and its rewards are fewer with each new Congress.

So far, two problems have been identified about the current system: that the transition between youth and adult is absurdly drawn out, and that youth and adult are the only two distinctions. Of course, one can reasonably argue that there are dozens of distinctions, like the legal ability to work, drive, join the military, sign a contract, rent an apartment, rent a car, be a victim of age discrimination, receive Social Security benefits, *etcetera ad nauseum*. Whether two or twenty-two divisions, the number hinders our society from functioning optimally.

These conundrums will be treated below, but there is also a third concern to the current approach, and that is its basis in age. Naturally, such is convenient, but any educator will corroborate the self-evident fact that age is a poor determinant of ability. The current education system employs *age-based batching* of children as they move through the grades, and they (and consequently we all) suffer tremendously because of it. Many precocious youths are ready for graduate-level education in their mid-teens, while many others will not reach that level of intellectual maturity until their mid-thirties. It is a great injustice to let age alone determine a child's classmates, just as it is equally unjust to make some youths wait until their eighteenth year to be accepted as adults, while accepting others *as early as* their eighteenth year. The convenience of age-based adulthood is a sorry excuse for its utilization.

The final consideration is, in a word, *expectation*. No person—stripling, adult, or elder—except those of preternatural internal drive—will rise much higher than the bar has been set. That is, people will seldom rise to a given level of maturity unless there is an expectation to do so. While relevant to every chapter of this book, it is especially poignant when discussing coming of age, particularly because there is crescive, but accelerating, implementation of new regulations that directly contradict this principle.

For example, what better sense will twenty-one-year-olds have than eighteen-year-olds if, in those three years, they are still treated like children? Drunkards at eighteen might rein in their behaviors by age twenty-one provided that they have been given the responsibility to do so, but denying the temptation those three years only delays the problem while compounding it with an additional three years of longing for forbidden fruit, sneaking it anyway, and reaping more severe consequences than are natural.

Furthermore, pushing so many things farther out serves to effectively punish responsible people—something that ought never be done—creating a self-fulfilling prophecy. People do not rise to challenges unless the challenges are there. If a young person is not permitted a glass of wine, then he cannot prove himself responsible, and thus the ascendancies will always say, "He is not ready." Whether at ten or twenty years, a driver's first experience behind the wheel is a shaky, fitful terror. The only way to avoid the learning curves of human experience is to avoid the experiences altogether, but that would be a contemptable solution.

Proposal of youth, adolescence, and adulthood

The first and foremost recommendation for improving the current state of affairs is to let adulthood have meaning. A streamlined system must not lengthen adulthood into a multi-year transition. Whether merit- or age-based (and, if age-based, whether at age fifteen or twenty-five), let there be a clear distinction. Let adulthood come with certain privileges and responsibilities hitherto denied, but now arrived all at once. An adult should never have to wait until some subsequent birthday to join the others who are further along. The transition into adulthood needs to be quick, decisive, and absolute.

Next, though feats of strength are better suited to a bygone era, the transition from childhood to adulthood should be accompanied by a rite of passage. Becoming an unabridged member of the citizenry ought to be attended by a solemn yet celebratory affair, complete with a full disclosure of one's new mandates, privileges, responsibilities, etc., followed by an attestation affirming understanding of the same. A courthouse or other public venue would suffice for such a ceremony whereat the community can welcome its newest full members. The event can be modest or grand but should in some ways feel like a graduation. After all, that's what it is, a graduation from childhood into adulthood.

Pertaining to childhood, the most sensible solution is to dichotomize it into youth (or true childhood) and adolescence (or juvenescence). Of the many reasons for this division, two are most compelling:

1. *The burden of benefits.* It is well and good to say, "anything for the children," but there is a practical limit to this. Additionally, one feels altogether differently about moving heaven and earth for a dependent five-year-old than for a twenty-year-old. Human instinct demands that we—individually and collectively—act self-sacrificingly toward children who cannot otherwise help themselves. The same human instinct is the opposite toward those who are well into their third decade and quite capable of pulling their own weight.

    We do not wish to see young children bound to their parents' fate nor beleaguered by the same hardships that burden them; as such, few people oppose the proposition that some public support be given to "our future," as it were. There is no cruelty in telling a thirty-year-old to pay for his own education or find a private benefactor who will, but it is another thing indeed to tell a child to teach himself to read because his parents cannot afford his education. The first is just; the second is unjust.

Therefore, society ought to invest in its youths, in seeing that they are fed, their medical needs attended, their illiteracy remedied. But this must happen *universally*—for all citizen-children regardless of their parents' circumstances—and *sensibly*—for only young children, because they are at the mercy of others. Truly, this is the best cause of any society's handouts and protections.

That said, just as raising a family is a burden to the household, caring for children is an enormous drain on the community's—the country's—resources. This does not mean that the burden is not worth the effort, but only that it is a Herculean effort indeed. As such, we must create a cutoff that is reasonably young and does not greatly disrespect the charity of the taxpayer. And as more and more assistances are lavished upon the nation's children, the more important that cutoff age becomes.

2. *The taunt of adulthood.* There is a great, long while between birth and adulthood, at whatever point it is set. In that time, the individual is gradually maturing and developing toward it. The yearning for it should be encouraged, not stifled. The desire for maturity and its prerogatives is akin to a child's innate desire for education:

A mathematics-loving child enjoys the rigors of the subject and requests more and more from her teachers. A good instructor pushes the child ever-so-slightly beyond her comfort level and allows her to chase that knowledge at whatever speed it comes naturally. Only a fool would tell a child who is ready for fractions that she must wait on her classmates who will be there in another year or so. By the time that she is finally allowed to move forward, her desire will have faded, and its fire reduced to dying embers.

In an analogous manner, when an adolescent who demonstrates responsibility, understanding, and maturity begins to crave adulthood, it ought to be given. Only insensibility and folly argue that he should wait another few years until his peers have caught up.

Under a better system, youths are entrusted with few privileges and few responsibilities, but they are given a kind and helpful hand from the collective society. Adolescents are entrusted with more privileges and responsibilities, and—in natural course—receive fewer handouts. Finally, adults are entrusted with high degrees of privilege and responsibility, and accordingly receive little public adminicle.

Qualifications

In a truly great world, age would not be a factor whatsoever. Age is only a bureaucratic "efficiency" in these matters; it is not a reflection of capabilities. Nevertheless, where perfection is unobtainable, we should settle for progress rather than stagnation; as such, some solutions must be incremental rather than complete. Thus, let the demarcation between youth and adolescence be around the average of puberty: say, age thirteen, which has the pleasing and concomitant advantage of delimiting the pre-teen years from those of the teenager. The transition from adolescence and adulthood should be roughly five to ten years later, depending on the individual.

Because adulthood is accompanied by serious responsibilities such as voting, owning businesses, owning land, and entering into legal contracts, not everyone will be ready at the same time. Those who have demonstrated objective maturity should be afforded the privileges much sooner than those who retain the trappings of youth. Consider the following proposed qualifications: An adolescent may apply for adulthood with proof of one or more of the following:

1. At least seventeen years old and serving in the military.

2. At least eighteen years old and having held a full-time job for at least one year.

3. At least nineteen years old and having graduated from a post-secondary institution.

4. At least twenty years old and currently enrolled in post-secondary education, having completed at least half of the graduation requirements.

5. At least twenty-four years old.

Though not accounting for many extraordinary circumstances nor a complete list of all worthy qualifications, note the progression of what has just been proposed. If one has been sworn into the United States military—having taken an oath to protect the country from its enemies or die trying, and sacrificing one's prime years of life to do so—then hasn't that person also earned the right to vote for those who will send the country to war, make his or her own medical decisions, and—of all things—drink a beer? Even if those people are merely seventeen years old, they have demonstrated greater responsibility and dedication to the country than many others ever will.

Not all eighteen-year-olds have been thrust into the real world and learned its first lessons, but if someone has been working a full-time job for over a year, then that person has at least evinced the ability to hold a job, earn an income, learn what precious-little spending power a dollar possesses, and—in many of those cases—support his or her own lifestyle.

Anyone who has stepped foot on a university campus will tell you that many of the individuals there—especially just beginning their programs—are a far cry from the more mature people they will be in a few short years. Their first semesters will be little different from high school—though probably a bit more boisterous—but their final semesters will be much closer to the impending self-supporting world of adulthood.

Now consider the last case that was set forth, or rather, think of the twenty-three-year-old who has not yet joined the workforce or military full time, nor has completed higher education, nor is even on track to do so. Has that person, who has spent a great deal of time doing who knows what, demonstrated that he is a responsible member of the community, who is invested in his and its wellbeing, who knows the value of a dollar, who is striving toward the values this country shares? With remarkably few extenuating exceptions, of course not. Yet one cannot stay a child forever, so let twenty-four be the last train to adulthood.

A brief apologia

This all might sound very harsh, but in truth, it is not. It is only asking that full-fledged membership into society be granted more thoughtfully than it currently is. Adulthood is accompanied by many responsibilities, some having enormous impacts on others. They should not be reserved for a council of wise elders, but neither should they be haphazardly thrown to so many who have not demonstrated capacity for it.

But a few points to regard:

1. The requirements of adulthood should not be so strict that they become a cudgel. Aside from making it burdensome to apply for adulthood—gathering large packets of paperwork that may or may not fulfill vague conditions, making it

very reminiscent of dealing with the DMV or IRS—strict requirements are poised to slide down their slippery slope and land in the colluvium of Jim Crow and other bigotry. *Responsible adults* are the goal—not oppression.

2. Adulthood needs to be naturally incentivized by the privileges that accompany its responsibilities. Adolescents should eagerly await adulthood, not attempt to delay it. If adulthood is allowed to have all the same restrictions of adolescence, only now with legal and other responsibilities, what's the point? It *would* be better to remain in adolescence for as long as possible. To avoid this possibility, adulthood must be accompanied by desirous liberties.

3. Adulthood would be of little use if its benefits were delayed until some future date. That is why the totality of legal, civil, social, and personal responsibilities must arrive all at once. Furthermore, it gives meaning to adulthood. When asking the question, "Am I allowed to . . .?" the answer is firmly *yes,* not, "Well, I am indeed an adult, but I won't be allowed to do such-and-such until such-and-such birthday." Those are the words of a child, not a self-responsible adult and full member of the community.

4. Closely related to the second point, adolescence cannot be accompanied by benefits that are unfit for the oldest of that category. For example, if you look at the table below, you'll notice that the privilege of operating motor vehicles is afforded to adolescents, but with the restriction of safety restraints. Society obliges a thirteen-year-old to use a seatbelt or motorcycle helmet because operation of a vehicle—though crucial and therefore

not denied—nevertheless has certain risks and safety concerns. An adult, on the other hand, is responsible for her own wellbeing and must choose her own safeguards. But a twenty-two-year-old adolescent who has not yet demonstrated the qualities of adulthood nor evinced enough maturity to make his own safety decisions is still very much like the thirteen-year-old, and they are accordingly grouped together.

On the other hand, while society might feel obligated to bestow certain benefits to a thirteen-year-old, such as covering a portion of her educational or medically necessary expenses, we have to ask if we would feel equally agreeable doing the same for a twenty-three-year-old. In most cases, the answer would be no, for one cannot—in good faith—make such a case to one's fellow citizens nor ask them to finance an individual who does not display any motivation to support himself.

5. I mention this as a point of prolepsis, for it is no doubt on the mind of many readers. Why is parenthood not a qualifier for adulthood? That viewpoint being, "Well surely someone with children should be an adult. After all, how can a child be responsible for a child?" The rebuttal is that, although young parents often discharge their duties admirably—shouldering great burdens and supporting their children no differently than older parents do—the act of having a child, in and of itself, does not guarantee adult behavior. Namely, some young parents effectively relinquish the majority of their children's care to other family members or rely heavily on government aid for the children's wellbeing. Though such situations are experienced for a variety of reasons, some of which are out of the parent control and, in any case, rarely

discount the difficulty of parenthood and its manifold strains, they nevertheless do not positively demonstrate the maturity, responsibility, and self-support expected of adults who influence and dictate—through the vote and other means—how other people live their own lives.

Conclusion

Society would profit from dividing itself into three divisions rather than two (the *de jure* standard) or dozens (the *de facto* standard). Partitioning the population into youths, adolescents, and adults allows each group to have fitting privileges and responsibilities, while also abolishing the imprecise transition that currently separates children from adults. Using age as a determinant is—presently—a necessary flaw but should not be the only determinant. Adulthood, in particular, should have many qualifiers—some based in age, others in worthiness.

Examples of Distinctions Between the Groups

The following table, though by no means exhaustive, might be useful when envisioning how a system like the one described in this chapter could work.

	Youth	**Adolescence**	**Adulthood**
Qualifications	Younger than 13	Older than 13	• Age 17 + military • Age 18 + job for ≥ 1 year • Age 19 + graduated college • Age 20 + halfway through college • Age 24
Can operate motor vehicles	No	Yes, but with safety restraints	Yes
Can vote	No	No	Yes
Can hold civil office	No	No	Yes
Can work for a business not owned by own family	No	Yes	Yes
Can declare a healthcare surrogate	No (is legal guardian)	No (is legal guardian)	Yes
Can enter into legal contracts	No	No	Yes
Can have legal dependents	No	No	Yes

Can access or consume adult content	No	Yes, with permission from guardians and proprietors	Yes
Healthcare autonomy	Decided by legal guardians	Decided by legal guardians for life-threatening and other serious cases	Decided by self or healthcare surrogate
Eligible for benefits	Yes	No	No
Requires legal guardian	Yes	Yes	No
Requires a photo ID	No	Yes	Yes

CHAPTER 3
MARRIAGE

> *There ought to be two distinct kinds of marriage: one governed by the State with rules enforced on all citizens, the other governed by the Church with rules enforced by her on her own members.*
>
> ~C. S. Lewis, from *Mere Christianity*

> *In ancient Rome, marriage was a civil affair governed by imperial law. But when the empire collapsed, in the 5th century, church courts took over and elevated marriage to a holy union.*
>
> ~*The Week* staff, from "How Marriage has Changed over Centuries"

Causes of contention

Marriage is one of the oldest human institutions, qualified by a rich, complicated history. The various religions, cultures, and epochs of our race have all taken their stances on marriage. As such, it is understandable and perforce predictable how wedlock is constantly subjected to interpretations, debates, and clashing opinions from every conceivable faction of society.

The United States is an especially charged theater. Its eclectic population and resultant bevy of religions, including the multiform lack thereof, eventuate a mire of opinions. Who is eligible for marriage? To whom? How many? Who can declare the union? In what manner? What are its agreements? What is its stance on severability? The questions are endless but not invalid. They agree on one thing only—a nationally unified opinion is unlikely to emerge.

The difficulty of defining marriage is compounded by the high valuation of religious freedom in the US. Striving to allow all religions to practice uninhibited while, simultaneously, endeavoring to honor none of them nor ingratiate any specific praxes as law, inevitably assures that many will be dissatisfied with, if not affronted by, the national policy of tolerance. That policy, then, which contravenes certain religions or the principles of persons who have none, is harshly criticized for violating the country's attitude toward religion as enshrined in the Bill of Rights: "Congress shall make no law respecting an establishment of religion, or prohibiting the free exercise thereof."

∼

Most of the current system's misery is caused by an unavailing design that gives *legal* standing to a *religious* union. Then, because the legal institution is available to all, whereas the religious one is limited to only those allowed by the religion itself, the legal extension steps on the toes of what the religion holds sacred and under its own purview.

To give a specific example, when a Roman Catholic priest marries two people, he does so through Catholic authority in accordance with the pertinent doctrines of the faith. The country's current approach errs by regarding that religious union and accepting that the couple, which has been married by the Catholic priest, is now also *legally* bound. The government conflates the affairs of the state with those of the church. (The word *church* refers to all religions and their various bodies, not solely to Christian ones.)

Yet, that is only half of the complication. When non-Catholics undertake to unite themselves, either through another religion or through a purely civil proceeding, they are regarded as the same legal entity as the newlywed Catholics. This potentially offends the non-Catholics, and certainly perturbs the Catholics who view the union not as a mere legal venture but as a religious matter concerning God and their faith.

Lastly, the issue is not tidily divided into supporters of pro-Christian and contra-Christian marriages, as there are widespread disagreements over the quiddity of matrimony even among those who identify by that religion. Regardless, even if society were dimidiated into adherents of religion X and those who oppose it, and assuming that their views on the subject were incompatible, still there would be no happy way to resolve the matter.

Proposition of legal concords

In a land that values and alleges separations between church and state, it is unconscionable for the US to honor or dismiss a union created by the church. The prospect that clergy can create a legally recognized union between people is senseless. Legality is the bailiwick of the state. Similarly, it is equally opprobrious for the laws of the state to obstruct or forbid a church's own internal affairs. Religion is the province of the church.

If we're open-minded, then the solution is quite simple and beneficial to all. C. S. Lewis summarized it most effectively when he wrote, "There ought to be two distinct kinds of marriage." One should be legal, the other should be religious, and they should have no overlap whatsoever. The two institutions argued for herein are called *marriage* and *legal concord*.

Let marriage be a strictly religious affair that the government cannot influence, sanction, restrict, or respect. Let it also have no legal standing whatsoever. Once liberated from legality and the opinions of non-adherents to the faith, each religion can design marriage according to its own precepts, including criteria for participation and termination.

Let legal concords, then, be altogether separate from marriage, as strictly legal affairs over which religion has no influence. Once loosed from religious influence, the government can establish policies and procedures that best suit the citizenry.

Marriage is entered into by whatever method the religion establishing it prescribes, and the union is severed under circumstances permitted by the same. Legal concords, likewise, are established and dissolved by whatever methods the state alone deems fit.

Note, especially, that the proposition of distinct marriages and legal concords does not prescribe one thing for religious persons and another for the non-religious; rather, marriages and legal concords exist in parallel, and one couple can engage in both simultaneously. Marriages are for the religious, and concords are for all.

Those who value their religion but abhor the government might choose to be married only. Those who have no religion but seek the legal conveniences of concords will likely engage in a legal concord but never seek to marry. And, certainly, many people will choose to participate in both—enter into marriage through a religious body and separately enter into a legal concord through the government.

Specifics of legal concords

Each religion is its own master, and it is therefore unwise—if not impossible—to remark upon the business of marriage. However, since legal concords are a matter of government, and since their proceedings are subject to the legislative and judicial processes, they are worth envisioning.

A legal concord is, in essence, a contract. As noted previously, legal concords are not administered by religious officials; authorized representatives of the government conduct them. Whether by lawyers, judges, or clerks, it makes no difference; legal concords are completely disparate from marriages and ought to be thought of as such.

The power of a legal concord, and its appeal to many, is its legal practicality: It is fundamentally an incorporation of various contracts that already exist. As a contract, it can be entered into by any two consenting adults who assume the following relationship: By definition, each member of a legal concord is the other member's beneficiary, healthcare surrogate, power of attorney, and obliged legal and financial partner. There could, of course, be other attributes, but these are the most essential.

There is no great mystery to the situation. If two people wish to be legally bound, then a legal concord accomplishes that purpose. Restricting these to exactly two individuals—not one, not three—is for practicality only: Healthcare surrogates, powers of attorney, etc. can only function properly with a single primary designee.

Being materially a simplification—that is, a one-stop-shop for many legal privileges that could otherwise be achieved separately—a legal concord should not be fragmented by picking and choosing its attributes. It is all or nothing. Two people cannot pursue a legal concord but desire to exclude each other as powers of attorney. If that is the desire, they can separately engage in all constituent contracts except for the displeasing ones. A legal concord is meant as a convenience not only for its members, but for the society around them. A medical professional should be confident that each member of a legal concord is the unconditional healthcare surrogate for the other. In the same way, a financial institution will know that an account in the name of one partner is, implicitly, in the names of both.

Speaking further on convenience, a legal concord cannot manifest its full potential until it becomes a nationally unified policy. As noted in the Introduction, laws ought to be implemented sparingly. Legal concords, however, are most effectively employed at the national level. Although generally each state in the US should safeguard its sovereignty from the nation as a whole, the legal concord is a quintessential exception to that rule. A national standard, in this case, is in the citizenry's convenience and best interest. Since marriage and legal concords are perfectly distinct and one cannot influence the other nor vice versa, a nationwide policy is not very imposing.

Implementation and civil unions

As with any proposal in this book and any proposal of any kind, there is always a question of *implementation*. Particularly, in this case, what would happen to the millions of couples who are currently married? Here, the path of least resistance is also the best. For those who are currently married, unless they wish it to be otherwise, their marriages, which are described by marriage licenses, should become legal concords. The religious aspect of their marriages should be addressed by the various religions to which they ascribe. Moving into the future, the distinction between marriage and legal concord should begin at once.

Lastly, to its credit, the government has attempted to make a religion-free version of marriage, namely, *civil union*. These contracts are failures, however, because they ignore the fundamental issue of marriage—mixing church and state. So long as religious proceedings are given legal credibility, and so long as civil servants can sanction unions that are a church's business, there will never be an agreeable resolution. Until there is a complete separation of the two, civil unions will always be seen as a half-hearted attempt to sidestep the real points of contention.

CHAPTER 4
LAND TENURE

> *The moment the idea is admitted into society that property is not as sacred as the laws of God, and that there is not a force of law and public justice to protect it, anarchy and tyranny commence.*
>
> ~John Adams

> *I [would] give a thousand furlongs of sea for an acre of barren ground.*
>
> ~William Shakespeare, from *The Tempest*

PROPERTY DEEDS ARE consummate expressions of self-actualization: muniments that represent security, possibility, independence, and the quintessence of humankind's desire to master its fate. Yet, the seemingly unlimited possibilities of land ownership are belied by each plot's inextricable connections to its neighbors, and those to theirs, until it becomes plain that a given landowner cannot sufficiently isolate his or her holdings. Therefore, the exacting task of society and its lawmakers is to safeguard as much freedom-of-property as can be reasonably tendered while simultaneously ensuring that such freedom does not appreciably violate the land of others.

Types of land ownership

Of ownership, there ought to be three broad classifications—private, commercial, and government. Though each of these should have commonalities, their distinctions are more important, as noted herein.

Private land is tenured by an individual. The people's interest in such land is familial security, stake in community, and the ability of each such landowner to strive toward self-sufficiency and abundance. Those who own land are invested in its physical location and, by and large, seek to better the community surrounding it. On one's own land, there should be few restrictions. Unless certain actions substantially disrupt the quality of the surrounding area, there is no just ground for prohibition.

Commercial land is tenured by a business. The people's interest in such land is growth, enterprise, employment, progress, production, and all other forms of industry that have made our society astir and abundant. Such land-owning businesses are, like private landowners, often invested in their physical locations and incentivized to better their surrounding communities. Depending on the use of such land, restrictions can reasonably vary between light and severe, as coffee shops and power plants are vastly disparate entities.

Government land is tenured by the various partitions of government—local, state, federal. The people's interest in such land is that it serves the citizens, be it public playgrounds, roads, courthouses, military bases, national parks, undeveloped land, etc. At the end of the day, such land exists not for its own sake, but because the citizenry has collectively asserted that its existence somehow serves the common good.

Private land, purchase and obligations

The transfer of private land—from seller to buyer—ought to be, like all exchanges of private property, a closed-door affair. The sale or gift should happen in whatever way the constituent parties decide, with this notable exception: Transfer of the title should occur at a courthouse with both the seller and buyer present, each of whom will pledge agreement to transfer terms before an appropriate government representative. The seller must hold the deed or have power of attorney over it so that the property, thereafter, can be confidently owned by the buyer. Courthouse proceedings—simple, yet definitive—including filing the new deed, should be free of charge for all parties involved, as land ownership is a valued aspect of liberty-loving societies.

There must be a clear, decisive way to verify that land is changing hands between the appropriate people, and that the seller indeed has the authority to sell it. To accomplish this, the previously described transfer between seller and buyer should take place. Additionally, the municipality in which the property is located should keep a record of provenance for each plot of land; this would describe the land and its owner as a timeline, so that the seller's claimed ownership of the deed can be easily validated, and so that the buyer's new claim to the land can be confidently asserted. The purpose of this procedure is to obviate the rampant contention of property ownership that currently plagues society.

As to the exotericism of a property's sale, there is no justifiable reason that it be public knowledge. When a title transfer happens, a new deed is filed with the government, and that property's provenance is updated. However, though a property's ownership is known by the government, the deed and provenance themselves should not be made public. Indeed, the only public knowledge about private land should be its classification as *private* and the geographical boundaries that define it. The current owner, previous owners, dates of sale, prices of those sales, etc. should be kept from public records to ensure the owners' privacy and—more importantly—safety.

Any exchange of land must be complete, total, and unrestricted. To ease society's burdens, avoid unexpected lawsuits, and impart a sense of security to a landowner, the purchased property must invariably include all structures and resources, including water, oil, minerals, timber, agriculture, etc. It is nonsensical that a plot of land and that which is upon or within it can belong to different people. If a property owner wishes to relinquish his or her claim to, say, the land's timber, then that must be separate from discussion about the land per se, and as a lease between those two parties only, without any obligation to future owners.

Accordingly, a current landowner should have no obligations established by the former. For example, if timber rights had been leased by the previous owner, that lease cannot pass to the new owner, and if the new owner wishes to create an identical situation with the lessee, then a new lease must be created. The current system allows for various property rights—particularly around oil and minerals—to be severed from the property itself, but this ignominious practice burdens current and future owners with the obligations of the previous ones. Worse still, many properties are sold without any knowledge of whether such rights have been severed and, if so, to whom.

In addition to oil, mineral, timber, air, and water rights, are concerns about other types of leases. For example, allowing a company to build a communications tower on one's property. If that property is sold, then the new owner should have complete authority with respect to allowing the tower to remain and, if so, under what conditions.

All burdens should be upon the bounden seller so that the buyer is liberated from them unless he or she engages in new leases, makes new promises. Therefore, if any portion of property is leased to another—whether to a student renting a spare room, a logger utilizing the timber, or a telephone company running wire across a field—the property owner/lessor must provide at least one year's notice to the lessee before ending the lease, or—necessarily—selling the property, at which time all leases must be concluded. And if a landowner engages in longer leases—say, promising mineral rights for five years—then that landowner does so with the understanding that the land cannot be sold before the lease has terminated.

Private land, rights and privileges

Landownership is an integral component of a free society, in part because a landowner has large autonomy over that land. First and foremost, the necessities of life should never be restricted or prohibited. Many municipalities employ specious arguments to forbid necessities such as collecting water or generating electricity, or to lade the manner in which they are done, but these are grave injustices that truncate liberty and force dependence on the state—ideas which contradict the very pith of landownership itself.

Providing for life's imperatives should never be inhibited; therefore, landowners should be able to engage in the following activities without impediment: to collect, store, purify, utilize, or consume water; to generate or store electricity; to store or stockpile food, fuel, provisions, equipment, or other victuals; to strengthen, fortify, or reinforce the property or its components; and more.

These activities and others like them should be restricted only when the activity itself would appreciably deteriorate the surrounding properties. For example, every landowner must have a right to collect water, but not at a volume that far exceeds even the most liberal allowance, to the point where one acre's worth of land depletes an aquifer that would otherwise provide for hundreds of acres. Similarly, every landowner must have a right to generate power, but not to create an industrial-scale, smoke-bellowing, coal-burning facility. There are reasonable limits and, if needed, restrictions to the rights and privileges of private land, but they must never become so suffocating that authorizations, approvals, and inspections are needed, or that one be entirely forbidden from collecting rainwater to prepare for the possibility of a drought, installing solar panels to continue on through a blackout, or keeping several gallons of gasoline in a shed to weather storms, be they snowstorms or supply-chain breakdowns.

Another obligation of life is a dwelling-place. Therefore, the construction of these too—that is, homes and other buildings—must not be unduly hampered. Building codes are important accessibility and safety checks on commercial and government land, but they are wholly inappropriate limitations where private land is concerned. Except as noted, one should be able to raise, modify, or destroy any structures on his or her land, as that person sees fit. The government has no justifiable authority to mandate that the doorframes in one's dwelling be a certain height or width, or that insulation is not too thick or too thin. Even concerning safety, it is entirely up to the landowner—the homeowner—how many smoke detectors to install and where, whether railings on a staircase are desirous, whether a deck should be hurricane-proof, or if an addition to the building is desired, and, if so, to what quality of construction. In short, on private land, building codes and inspections are best practices only; they ought to be voluntary, and those who reject them ought to be able to do so without fear of consequence, discrimination, or marginalization. Indeed, permits, applications, authorizations, and other such regulatory processes are improper for private land.

However, there are exceptions to this freedom. Building codes, for example, are necessary to obviate cases in which a landowner's noncompliance with otherwise voluntary building codes can reasonably endanger the property or persons of others who do not directly interact with that land. Common concerns include *environmental hazards* such as sewage, groundwater infiltration, topsoil erosion, or *safety hazards*, such as flimsy roofs or egregious fire risks.

For example, if two houses upon two different properties are nevertheless a stone's throw from each other, and the owner of house A does not property secure that dwelling's roof, then it is likely that a bad storm will send debris from house A crashing into house B. In this case, both homeowners, as members of a cooperative society, have mutual obligations to each other to build sound homes compliant with reasonable standards. If, on the other hand, another house—house C—is built hundreds of yards away from another's property, then there *does not exist* a *reasonable* possibility that the roof of house C will affect anyone other than the inhabitants of that house. Therefore, house C should not be subject to building codes.

One final consideration of the rights and privileges accorded to private property: Any intrusions upon such rights ought to bear their own burden of assertion. The default assumption is that all liberties are inherent to private property and thereby unrestricted. Therefore, all restrictions are assumed to be inappropriate and beyond the state's authority unless they can be proved necessary. For example, it is assumed that one can dig a hole in his or her own land; if that right is to be removed, then someone must prove why that hole, or any, violates the property of another. Unless that argument is proved, the hole can be dug.

In this light, there are certain fundamental, immanent, inherent property rights that are abused but ought to be buttressed. To enumerate a few: Private property cannot be photographed—from ground, air, or space—by a commercial entity without the expressed consent of the owner. Furthermore, private property is not to be burdened by low-flying aircraft, manned or unmanned. Plants, animals, and people can be restricted from entering the property, and removed—after sensible warning—if found upon it. No agent can mandate that telephone lines, streetlights, power lines, aqueducts, pipelines, etc. be placed upon private land.

There are many more, but the most noteworthy is that a landowner has the right to quality of life. No single-family house should have to fear that its neighboring house will be sold to a developer who will construct a twenty-story high-rise in its place. Such urbanizing construction is an integral part of our progressive society, but it should never happen at the expense of those who lack the means to fight such insidiousness. Private land tenure is constituent of a free, resilient society, and, accordingly, it ought to be valued as such.

Commercial land

Commercial land should enjoy many of the safeguards applied to private ownership. Nevertheless, the two have notable differences. First and foremost, commercial land primarily accommodates business purposes, which can range wildly from storefronts to hospitals, farms to warehouses, manufacturing facilities to office space, and far beyond these. In all cases, however, the land is owned by a business rather than an individual, even if a sole proprietor manages that business.

The deed to commercial land should be managed and transferred in the same fashion to private owners. The notable difference is that the ownership of commercial land should be public knowledge and reasonably accessible to whoever might seek that knowledge. Still, the details of these title-transfers is the private affair of the parties involved; the final selling-price, negotiation history, business representatives, other arrangements, etc. are the privileged knowledge of the buyer and seller, not to be disclosed publicly except by the entities themselves, if they are desirous to do so.

In contrast to private land, commercial land must abide by the building codes set forth by their respective municipalities. Such rules can be rigorous where necessary, but in every case should be reasonable and legislated in good faith.

Government land

Unlike the owners of private or commercial land, the government is not a true owner of the land it holds, but a custodian. As mentioned in this chapter's introduction, the visage of government land can vary from open wilderness to urban roads, libraries to military bases.

When considering the usage of public land, the government must thoughtfully consider the proposed purpose and how it affects the private and commercial land around it; the government's desires should always be guided by justice to individuals and the best interest of the population.

Where reasonable, government land should be freely accessible to the population, and explicit in its purpose. Top-secret military facilities are a counterexample because such places are beyond the scope of local government and should not, for obvious security and safety reasons, be public.

Eminent Domain

The final clause of the Fifth Amendment to the United States Constitution states "nor shall private property be taken for public use, without just compensation." The intent of such a statement is to protect private property from uncompensated government seizure. As with all societal affairs, there is a balance between individual liberty and collective good, yet to protect against cruel oppression and unbridled tyranny, procedures and legislation should err on the side of individual liberty. When then, should an individual be deprived of private property, and what restitution—if any—ought to be made? America's Founding Fathers sought to ensure that private property would never be taken without just compensation, but in the many years since, this safeguard has been sorely abused and, therefore, must be reassessed and bolstered.

Currently, private land can be seized from the owner with no greater reparation than its pitifully inadequate appraised value. Worse still, it can be taken for unconscionable purposes, often to satisfy a commercial entity such as a housing developer or energy company. Let property be inviolable, and let businesses acquire land honestly. Therefore, the first qualifier to eminent domain—expropriation, or the seizure of property—is that the confiscation must be proved absolutely necessary at multiple levels of government and before a jury of the deprived person's peers.

Next, we must ask, "What can be taken?" Naturally, we consider land, its resources, and the permanent structures that sit upon it, but what about vehicles, watercraft, aircraft, stockpiled resources, computers, technology, or the book you hold in your hand? Can this private property be taken for public use? *Should* it be?

To protect both individuals and businesses, eminent domain must be limited to only private and commercial *land*. Of course, when land is seized, so too are the structures upon it—whether private home or large-scale factory. Nevertheless, if the landowner chooses to damage, destroy, or otherwise degrade that which is being taken, then he or she ought to be able to do so without fear of reduced compensation or any other adverse repercussion. That which is needed and confiscated is, theoretically, the land itself and not the buildings upon it. If the government craves a building, then let it make an honest offer and attempt purchase like any other, and let it content itself if the offer is rejected. Land is the only property that can be rightfully subjected to eminent domain.

After the necessity of seizure has been inarguably established at multiple levels of government and before a jury of the deprived's peers, adequate notice of eviction must be provided. At least twenty-four months should suffice.

Finally, there is consideration of compensation which, in all cases, must be non-taxable. Several sources should be employed to determine the land's most liberal worth from the proceeding five years through the future five. The highest theoretical value during that ten-year span will be the land's appraised value.

For commercial land, the landowner's eviction orders must be accompanied by a lump-sum payment equal to one-and-a-half times the land's appraised value, plus 50 percent of the profit derived from that land from the previous eighteen months. Additionally, another payment of that 50 percent profit must be paid prior to the effective date of seizure. The total just compensation being at least twenty-four months' notice, 150 percent of the land's greatest theoretical worth at any point during the surrounding ten years, and 100 percent of the profit generated by that land from the previous eighteen months.

For private land, the landowner's eviction orders must be accompanied by a lump-sum payment equal to twice the land's appraised value. That same amount must be paid again prior to the effective date of seizure. To deter the government from confiscating land on behalf of commercial entities or with the intention of eftsoons selling the confiscated land, the landowner will, additionally, enjoy 10 percent of the gross revenue from the property's new use, paid at three-month intervals, for five years following the seizure and, lastly, the seized land may be neither owned nor commercialized by an entity other than the acquiring government for a period of no fewer than fifty years. The total just compensation being four times the land's greatest theoretical worth, 10 percent of the land's revenue for five years following seizure, and assurance that the land is confiscated for some honest public good.

∼

Eminent domain is warranted in certain—perhaps even in many—circumstances. But the price—in both money and moral outrage—must be severe, and the process tedious and inconvenient enough to cause the government great hesitancy. It must assert that its purposes justify desecrating the sanctity of private property, and once resolute in its proposed course of action, the government must make extravagantly generous returns to the victim of society's common good.

Miscellaneous improvements

In addition to that which has been set forth already, that which follows are additional ways in which land tenure can be modified to help create a better world:

1. For all land, the rights to resources should be returned to the landowners and, thereafter, severance of resources should be disallowed. To facilitate the transition, once this declaration is made, anyone claiming such rights on a property smaller than five acres must relinquish those claims. If the claim is to a larger property, then it must be filed within six months, and the burden of proof will fall to that claimant. If the claimant does indeed own the rights to certain resources on another's land, and the landowner and claimant cannot come to an agreeable resolution on their own, then it should be arbitrated before specialized courts established for this purpose. Moving forward, resource rights should be leased, as discussed above, and the land cannot change owners while a lease is active.

2. Each municipality should establish the undisputed owner of all land and authoritatively install a system for provenance. Claims to ownership must be established within six months of this declaration. Competing claims should then be arbitrated before specialized courts. Hereafter, the aforementioned procedures of transferring ownership should be abided so that landownership will be certain. After this, absurdities such as title insurance will be irrelevant.

3. Because land usage so thoroughly commands the destiny of its circumambient canton, only those entrusted to decide the course of that territory should be allowed to tenure its land. In a perfect world, landowners would be obliged to their land and, subordinately, to their community, thereby motivated to improve the place rather than exploit it then abandon. But in practice, a comparable safeguard is to restrict private landownership to the citizenry and commercial landownership to businesses based in the country itself.

4. A more thorough discourse on taxation can be found in the chapter about the same, but to mention the features pertinent to land tenure. In the absence of other taxes, it is reasonable to levy demesne tax on landholdings. For a given large swath of land—say, a zip code or county—such a tax should consider only acreage, that is, within that large area, every landowner is taxed the same amount per acre, regardless of the quality of that land, the improvements made to it, the structures built upon it, the estimated worth or revenue of the person owning it, or any other factor. An acre of land is an acre of land, not its proximity to desirable areas, nor the quality of the buildings upon it, nor the quality of its neighboring properties have any

justifiable consideration in its tax rate. All landowners should be taxed the same for the same acreage in the same vicinity.

Furthermore, the tax rate must not increase by more than a maximum of three and a half percent annually. At this limit, property tax will not double more frequently than once every twenty-one years. This slow increase prevents those of lower and middle income from suddenly being forced from their land due to industrialization, emigration, gentrification, growing population, or any other phenomenon which suddenly skyrockets property values.

CHAPTER 5

CONSUMER RIGHTS

> *Wrong does not cease to be wrong because the majority share in it.*
>
> ~Leo Tolstoy, from *A Confession*

> *Our liberties we prize, and our rights we will maintain.*
>
> ~Motto of the State of Iowa

BUSINESS, PURELY AND of its own accord, is difficult enough, but when embattled by overwhelming taxation and regulation, viability becomes tenuous, and companies are compelled to seek revenue from unconventional sources such as selling personal information. Consequently, a vast collection of corporations across all industries now engages in collecting, storing, and monetizing information about people: employees, clients, customers, and whoever else is available. While many companies are still governed by ethical principles and led by honorable leaders, there are, nevertheless, strong trends in the opposite direction, and this and other sordid practices have become frighteningly widespread. However, it is a great deception to contend that prevalent practices are wholesome practices, as Saint Augustine succinctly expressed when he wrote, "Right is right, even if no one is doing it; wrong is wrong, even if everyone is doing it."

Violating human rights is profitable, ubiquitous, and integral to the current economy. These take various forms, none of which are insignificant, but herein the topic is limited to violations of basic consumer rights, especially personal information. Safeguarding consumer rights (or any human rights) will unquestionably shake the world's economy . . . but only temporarily. As the abolition of slavery unsettled and disarrayed that institution's dependent economies, more virtuous industries arose from their ashes. Such changes are ferociously unwelcomed by those who are reliant upon vicious practices, but the quality of our society depends upon eradicating injustice regardless of its prevalence, profitability, or legality.

Personal information

Many companies engage in the monetization of others' personal information because it is profitable, because their peers do the same, and because it is not expressly illegal. Vague business-related needs defend these practices—comprehensive profiles help the business better serve its customers, more information allows for more robust validation or security, and other rote sophistry. The actions are then upheld by insensate legalities such as privacy agreements, terms of use, checkboxes, asterisks, *caveat emptor* (buyer beware), and "You should have done your due diligence." For simplicity, we can refer to all such documents as *privacy agreements* and note three prominent faults: they are jargonistic, vague, and support unvirtuous causes.

First, as contracts, privacy agreements abound with legalese and other industry-specific jargon that is unintelligible to the average person. Lengthy concordats might be appropriate when two large companies merge, but they are out of place when purchasing trinkets or viewing webpages. Standard business interactions have no need for legally watertight ententes, and there is no measure of reason that allows for consumers to encounter such documents and be bound by them in any way.

Implied agreement to such contracts with the click of every button, or even by simply having passed it by, is akin to posting a ten-page, small-font document in a storefront window and telling each person who enters that he or she is now bound by its terms. The proposition is lunacy, and yet the current system has declared, "They are so bound." Yet, even if each shopper *were* to stop and read that which was posted, most of them would be hard pressed to understand it. The average passerby is not an expert on law, neither is he expected to seek legal counsel to understand it, as if patronaging a business were the same as negotiating the sale of many copyrights.

Secondly, if the consumer in good faith reads the entire privacy agreement and understands its nuanced jargon, the actual content is laughably vague. When the rubber meets the road, no specific who, what, where, or anything is concretely stated, at least not without concluding items like *and others* or *etc.* or *reserve the right to change without notice*.

What information is being collected? Personal information such as name, location, or other sundry information you provide intentionally or unwittingly. What are the terms and conditions? Those of the company, and any of its unspecified third parties. What is the justification? Unmentioned applicable laws.

Finally, though some information might be gathered with good intentions, privacy agreements create no barriers between good and ill. These documents are written to provide maximum latitude to the corporations that use them, so that anything and everything can be gathered without consent, utilized without impediment, stored without inconvenience, retained without timeline, sold without consideration, and resisted without effect.

Legislators who claim to respect an individual's right to personal information have designed nothing better than laws that allow a consumer to somehow contact unfindable people at these companies and request that they furnish less-vague lists of all that which the privacy agreements enumerate. But how does a truly better world look?

In the short-term, we must create legislation that, within a reasonable period—say, six months—requires all companies to contact the people whose information they have, tell them which data points exist, and ask for confirmation that it should be retained. If a person cannot be contacted or does not reply positively, then the data must be quickly deleted or destroyed.

Moving forward, these courses of action must be supplemented by legislation that prevents companies from obtaining information without the expressed consent of the person whose information it is. Of that which is collected, companies must enumerate the information they intend to keep, as well as the method through which it will be obtained, before services are engaged, and each piece of information must be agreed upon. For example, while creating an account, you are told that the company will keep your full name, email address, phone number, and IP address, and unless you actively consent to these, the permission is denied.

Consumers must also be told how, where, and by whom their information will be stored and used. For example, that it will be stored on company-owned servers in Virginia, and managed and accessed only by the company's employees. Also, that the information will be used to identify one's account, and it will be deleted within thirty days of the account's deletion.

Third parties and their uses of information must also be provided and consented to. New third parties and new uses naturally warrant updated consent—that each consumer chooses to accept the changes or part ways with the company. Additionally, there should be convenient ways for consumers to request their own information or have it speedily destroyed, deleted, or anonymized.

While at first glance these suggestions can seem overwhelming, they are actually modest and practicable. Indeed, if a business has information on people, then it can attempt to reach out to them. As to the business losses that will arise from possibly deleting so much data, the comparison to slavery is once again appropriate. Profitability does not make it correct, and loss of those profits is an acceptable sacrifice if it furthers human rights.

Furthermore, though businesses may claim to own this data or have obtained it rightfully, neither is true. Even if both premises are legal, they lack moral standing and goodwill. Just as murder is wrong and ought to be punished regardless of lawmakers' views about it, so too are affronts to privacy and personal information. Policies permitting these abuses need to be amended, even at great cost and effort.

When interacting with a business

Generally, there is more to a consumer's relationship with a business than the information that business keeps. While each business should have a wide berth for its own policies, there are a few grossly abused, unprotected consumer entitlements that are worth addressing, for which appropriate legislation should be ratified.

Entitlements, as categorized here, are somewhere between inalienable rights and nice-to-haves. Inalienable rights are weighty, inherent, and never justifiably abridged. Nice-to-haves are pleasing practices that nevertheless can't be forced upon anyone. Entitlements, however, are expected and deserved, yet not irrefragably constitutional to the fabric of society.

Entitlement to customer service. Too many companies hide behind insufficient customer service and avoid customer obligations. Consumers should have the ability to communicate with the company in person, via mail, and through the company's primary means of communication. There should always be a discernable location to which one can physically go, or an address at which mail will be received, or a phone number that can be called, or email address and a *contact us* page on a website, etc.

Regardless of the channel, it must be easily found—not so hidden that the searching becomes tedious or effectively undoable. Once customer service is sought, responses should be timely—not hours or days away. Finally, it is imperative that, when requested, customers have access to people—not solely automation or artificial intelligence.

Entitlement to lack third-party products. Consumers have the reasonable expectation that they can patronize a business without first needing to patronize some other business. If it were otherwise, a few well-placed companies could become the de facto rulers of the world, forcing every participant of modern society to engage their services.

Consider the slippery slope of a retailer that refuses to sell eyeglasses to customers lacking prescriptions, so the customers are forced to find optometrists. Meanwhile, what if optometrists mandate insurance? Then what if insurance companies require email addresses? Wouldn't that require the use of the internet, an internet provider, and a company that purveys email accounts only after users are bound by vague privacy agreements? What's a purblind wretch to do?

But of course, the real world is far more subtle and insidious than this. And even if there is not a cabal of treacherous executives attempting to force a worldwide customer base, consumers should have the ability to participate in one business without needing something from another.

A growing example of such dependence on third parties is found in restaurants that have online-only menus that must be scanned from a phone while at the table. While convenient for many, what about those who lack smart phones or who cannot get signals or have dead batteries? Without alternatives, restaurants can create situations that perforce demand the use of third parties (cell phone companies, etc.) and marginalize those who do not or cannot utilize them.

Just as businesses need contingencies for the blind, deaf, and others who cannot engage conventionally, it is imperative that businesses also design contingencies for those who lack a cell phone, credit card, or other assumed third-party product.

Entitlement to deny unnecessary information. Because it helps them streamline business and improve services, many companies ask their customers for information that is not strictly necessary, such as a phone company asking for an email address. It is extremely difficult to make purchases, obtain medical services, find employment, or travel without first furnishing first name, last name, email, phone number, home address, and credit card. Ideally, nonessential information is voluntary, not required. For example, because medical treatment does not hinge on a patient's having or lacking an email, leaving that field blank should not disqualify a person from receiving care.

Entitlement to sever ties. For any number of reasons ranging from morality to absurdity and beyond, a person may wish to sever ties with an organization. He or she should be allowed to, without hassle. Currently, there are organizations that, citing internal policy and various regulatory laws, deny customer requests to delete or dispossess their information. As many companies can neither safeguard data nor resist the temptation to monetize it, consumers must have the ability to remove themselves and their information.

Entitlement to returns. In any business transaction, there is an implicit understanding that the customer is purchasing a given product or service as described. But what happens when size-ten shoes arrive at the door and are really size-seven? Or what about when a product is damaged? Most businesses have reasonable return policies, but others say tough luck because they already have the customer's money. The problem, however, is that while you—the customer—have fulfilled your obligation to pay, the business did not provide that which was promised.

Therefore, when the business does not abide by its half of the sale, the customer is entitled to a return. The full purchase price—including taxes, fees, shipping, and gratuities—should be returned quickly. Furthermore, in addition to whatever other means the business may choose, the customer must always have the option to receive cash. Some businesses offer only store credit, but that keeps money within the company and prevents customers from recovering their losses, contradicting the idea of a return.

Entitlement to pay cash. For good or ill, one of our society's foundations is government-sponsored currency. The promise of this fiduciary money is that the government's approved coins and banknotes are universally acceptable. Thankfully, modern technology and conveniences have led to a society in which one does not need to carry around stacks of cash but can usually prosper with less. At one point, *less* meant a checkbook; now, it means credit cards and phone apps. In the future, it will look different. But at the end of the day, the currency's promise is that its original expression—a coin or a bill—will be acceptable and legitimate.

Physical currency is important because, for all intents and purposes, it is facilitated by the government only. Alternatives, such as the aforementioned checkbook, credit card, and mobile app are convenient, yet they depend on third parties: banks, credit card companies, cell phone manufactures and application developers, etc. Universal acceptance of physical currency like cash creates reliability and safeguards freedom from third parties. Though cash can be inconvenient for certain businesses, the consequences of *not* accepting cash are far too deleterious. Therefore, the government that promises its currency's legitimacy must also ensure its acceptability.

Food and consumables

Even more egregious than abuses of personal information are, perhaps, the lack of knowledge consumers have about what they put into their bodies. And while it is arguable that a person can survive without the companies that affront their personal information, one cannot survive without food.

Food can be misleadingly labeled, but even more important is the information that is altogether lacking. If the following proposals were adopted, then people would know what they are putting into their bodies, and food industries would likely be driven to producing higher quality products.

1. **False advertising.** First and foremost, food cannot be deceptively labeled, such as marketing honey-flavored corn syrup as *honey*, cheese-plastic amalgamations as *cheese*, or minced corn-chicken-feather-feces mash as *chicken*. Such mislabeling is obviously intended to convince the consumer that the product is something other than what it actually is—a practice that is not only immoral but should be illegal.

2. **Ingredients.** All of a food's ingredients should be listed by proportion, including any unnatural admixtures such as plastic, synthetic fillers, and other substances.

3. **Treatments.** What was applied to the plant or animals while growing? Whether considered organic or not, the chemicals, pesticides, drugs, hormones, etc. that were

applied even before something became *food*, ought to be listed on the product.

4. **Food's food.** Plants are seldom grown without fertilizer, and no animal is grown without eating something. These should be listed.

5. **Origins.** Consumers must be told the origins of their food, when and how it was killed, picked, captured, or otherwise culled.

While these five details do not cover all the information that every consumer should have, their honest application would reveal almost everything that people need to make informed decisions about their health, environmental impact, and ethical obligations. Additionally, while mandating this information would not avert all of the unwholesome practices that the food industry employs, it would give consumers a fighting chance to *vote with their dollar* and direct their business where they feel most comfortable.

Vignette of a better world

Four years ago, you were in the hospital. Thankfully, you were sent home with a clean bill of health. Within one month of your discharge, a letter came in the mail, a twenty-question survey about your stay. You had been quite pleased with the staff, but less so with the room's cleanliness, so you completed the survey accordingly. You didn't think much about it because surveys are standard practice valuable channels for communicating with businesses.

Two years later, you noticed a surge of medically related junk mail, physical and electronic. Pharmaceuticals, medical-supply stores, drug stores, online discount companies, medical insurance, and seemingly everyone had an uncomfortable amount of your personal information. About a month later, you became a victim of identity theft. How did this happen? You are diligent to protect your information, shred your documents, and avoid suspicious websites. So, where was the leak?

It turns out that your *anonymous* healthcare survey wasn't truly anonymous. The hospital had violated your right to medical privacy when it gave a marketing-and-survey company your name, address, dates of stay, and the reason for your visit. Your hospital contracted the survey company for the stated purposes of improving care and safety, and that was the hospital's sincere intention. But the survey company had other plans for your responses.

Back in the day, when the company received surveys they protected respondents by anonymizing their feedback. More recently, as the economy grew tougher, company executives decided that data did not only *supplement* the company's products, but that data *itself* could be a product, so it adopted the latest business models for monetizing customer information.

First things first, they survey company dismissed any legal hurdles. Although the data came from a healthcare source and is—supposedly—protected under law, because the information itself was not about medical treatment, it did not qualify for that protection. It was perfectly legal for the company to obtain, store, and utilize your data.

At first, the survey company didn't know what it would do with your information, but it knew that there was value in it. Your medical stay, name, and contact information didn't reveal much, though, so it was supplemented. Like many of its industry peers, the company exchanged its data for subscriptions to the repositories of several major internet browsers. That supplemental information allowed the survey company to create a comprehensive profile on you. With your internet browsing history, they learned your location, previous addresses, travel history, daily habits, associates, interests, and so much more.

The survey company then sold your profile to nationwide medical retailers, as well as the hospitals in your area, all of which created targeted advertisements and sent them to you.

That harassment, however, was little compared to the horrors of attempting to recover your identity. Dozens of companies had more information about you than you knew about yourself, and the truth is that it would have been more secure nailed to your front door, because most of them used third-party servers managed by big-tech companies from around the world. Even under ideal circumstances, any one of them could have been breached—and one of them was.

You fit all these pieces together only after new legislation that placed high value on privacy and strict restrictions on businesses. Shortly before it was enacted, you were again at the hospital, discharged in good health, and given a survey in the mail, which you again kindly completed and returned. But due to the new laws, you received another letter in the mail—one of many. It was from the survey company, reluctantly disclosing that they had a comprehensive profile about you; there were over two-hundred individual data points, including extensive financial data, your passport number, your alma mater, your college major, your children's names and dates of birth, and even your estimated daily caloric intake. The letter invited you to check a box next to each piece of information the survey company wished to retain, but you didn't check a single one.

In your more naïve days, you feared that someone might stumble upon your credit card statement in the recycling bin. Never in a million years had you suspected that a marketing-and-survey company was stealing and selling your data. But that was then. Now, it's a better world, and there are protections against those evils.

So many things are better these days. Last month, when you bought a size medium sweater online, which upon opening was actually extra small, you were able to return it without hassle. Previously you would have had to make an exchange or accept store credit, but since you've had several similar incidents with that retailer, you took the cash and walked away.

You're also in better health now that you know what you're eating. For years you thought you were eating pure tuna for lunch, but with the new food regulations, you found out that "100-percent tuna" really means half tuna meat and half edible plastic. You also realized that the fish were caught over three years before reaching you, using techniques you disapprove of. Now, you choose a better brand.

Finally, you no longer receive weekly junk mail from that credit company. You had applied for a new credit card, but they denied you because of an outdated address. However, they then sent you applications in the mail several times a month. One day, you finally called customer service and asked them to stop sending you mail. When a similar thing happened before legislation banned the practice, you waited on-hold for two hours and were finally told that they couldn't find your account. But under new regulations, you were able to call the new company, get through to someone almost immediately, and tell them to delete your data. A week later, you received a confirmation letter in the mail, and you haven't been pestered since.

You wonder why it took so long for these policies to be implemented. The previous state of affairs was appalling. But now you command your own information. You feel better knowing that you're not helplessly at the mercy of corporate policies. When they send you the wrong product, you can get your money back; when you need to speak to someone, you can; when you hear rumors that they misuse your data, you call them up and have them delete your account and any record of it. You know what's in your food and where it came from. On the whole, things are improving. You're living in what feels like—and now is—a better world.

CHAPTER 6

HEALTHCARE

> *America's health care system is neither healthy, caring, nor a system.*
>
> ~Walter Cronkite

> *Ignorance is king. Many would not profit by his abdication. Many enrich themselves by means of his dark monarchy. They are his Court, and in his name they defraud and govern, enrich themselves and perpetuate their power.*
>
> ~Walter Miller, from *A Canticle for Leibowitz*

WHEREAS ENERGY IS largely an issue of science, welfare of charity, disaster relief of resources, and effective legislation of ethics and moral theory, healthcare is the union of all these concerns, and more. In a better world, one in which the healthcare system flourishes, the medical system would represent the crowning achievement of a wholesome society, for it would sit—fulfilled—at the intersection of humanity's proudest virtues and hardiest capacities. Yet even in a lesser world, healthcare still remains at the connection of all these things, and perhaps that is the source of its difficulty.

When society is led assiduously by ideals, then healthcare

thrives and is itself idyllic, yet when the opposite is true, the healthcare system reflects that corrupting infection. Unfortunately, the current state is this: Where people should be embraced, they are rejected; where there should be hope, there is fear; where solutions should be collaborative and creative, they are dictatorial and bureaucratic. Any and all who have interacted with the greater medical services can unite around the need for change. That unity is shattered, however, when the conversation is limited to the role of medical insurance and its proper scope. Indeed, of all the many industries that must cooperate to deliver quality medical care, insurance is one of the few that is not actually inherent to the mission. Despite its limited utility, insurance has not only crept its way into conversations about change but has been lifted up as the only worthwhile topic.

While medical insurance can have a part to play in improving healthcare, its ability to help is fundamentally limited by its nonexistent role in treating patients. Scientists advance knowledge, engineers development equipment, educators train others, clinical staff treat patients, laborers sustain the infrastructure, and philanthropists help fund the process, yet arguments about insurance have supplanted serious consideration of all these others who do have the potential to contribute in a way that leads to meaningful change. Because medical care concenters a vast panoply of our society—a diverse assortment of all that mankind holds dear and has created to uphold—it demands sweeping, interdisciplinary solutions. To keep the focus narrowly upon insurance is a disservice to every member of our society and belies our very ability to accomplish good works.

What we need, then, is a new conversation. Although this book strives to offer the practical advice promised by its title, the solutions to healthcare will not be found in these pages. Notwithstanding, the following content is intended to help foster conversation on a few key topics.

Effect of insurance

Everyone wants universal healthcare, or so we presume, in the pure sense of it. Rarely is anyone so heartlessly callous as to forbid decent medical care. Like access to clean water and nutritious food, no one really wishes to deny these things to anyone else. Lines are drawn and flags planted in the sand, not about the ideals themselves, but about the modes of attaining them or their feasibility altogether. Medical care is no different. Universal, uninhibited access to it would be great, but we must first wrestle with the question of whether or not such is possible and, if so, the unintended consequences of its fruition.

One of the boldest lies of our era is that medical insurance equates to accessible medical care. Not only this, but the contrapositive too—that without medical insurance, then there can be no medical care, accessible or otherwise. Both statements are falsehoods—blatant lies, if you will. The easiest way to understand why is to note that insurance has nothing to do with developing or rendering treatment. Its only bailiwick is payment. At best, therefore, insurance is but one tool of the many used to fix the machine, but it is not a magical, all-in-one tool, nor, frankly, a very useful one.

Above all else, though, it is important to understand the limitations of insurance. Believing that it is a catholicon cure-all for the healthcare system will only lead us very far down an unfulfilling road. Chasing after insurance will cause us to ignore genuine resolutions. Worst of all, though, it will cause bitter resentment between those who chase after it and those who do not. Remember, all people support the goal of abundant, affordable, accessible medical care. Insurance is not the end, but a proposed means. Now, then, let us consider that means and some of its consequences.

Mythology states that when Pandora opened her box, horrors were unleashed into the world, and they could not be contained again. More recently, atomic weapons were developed, though humanity wishes that they never had been. Now we must wrestle with how to handle something we wish had never been conceived. The same could be said about insurance—oh, that it was never invented.

The danger of insurance is not its nuclear fallout, but a far more insidious radiation, one which has suffused across our culture and imbedded itself deep within. Its peril is presented as its benefit—removing the payer from the payment. This sounds good because medical bills are very expensive. If insurance—not patients—covers the bills, then all people, no matter how financially strained, can receive medical care. Of course, though, this is not really the case. Insurance is a street magician. Its slight-of-hand is subtle, but if we pay attention, we can spot its legerdemain and expose the truth of it.

First, insurance does not remove payment from the patient. Currently, insurance has monthly fees, usually for both the insured and his or her employer, also deductibles, out-of-pocket expenses, copays, coinsurance, and a bevy of other jargon designed to obfuscate the cost and whoever is responsible for it. Indeed, insurance is not cheap. Even if the government or another entity were to give everybody insurance for *free*, the cost would merely be hidden. Employers hide that cost by paying their workforce lower wages; the government hides it through greater taxation. Either way, the patient pays for it.

But does the patient pay the full amount? That is to ask whether insurance still saves money for the patient? Yes and no. Yes, in the sense that the patient only pays a percentage of the bill, for indeed insurance does pay on behalf of the insured. No, in the sense that the bill has been artificially inflated to account for insurance. It is the same as a merchant taking a four-dollar item, raising its price to eight dollars, and then selling it for half off. After spending four dollars, did you really save four? But in reality, it is more like that merchant raising the price to twelve dollars, charging a two-dollar monthly membership fee, and then offering members a 25 percent discount if the member can demonstrate a convincing need for it and has already spent two-hundred dollars within the calendar year. Sadly, that scenario is comparably rudimentary to the actual complexities involved.

However, the real danger comes threefold: First, when it is not one gimmicky merchant greasing this scheme, but when all businesses must legally employ such tactics. In that case, one cannot choose the honest merchant over this ignominious one. Instead, we're forced to gain membership with someone somewhere or be forced to buck up and pay twelve dollars for that item which would have—in a different world—been merely four. Second, it is not the merchant—that is, the hospital, the physician's office, etc.—who devised this scheme, for they are as appalled as the customer. Rather, a third party has placed the burden, so it is not easily removed.

The third danger is that whenever payment is removed from the payer and placed elsewhere, prices rise. This is true of any insurance. Consider homeowner's insurance and the price of roofs. Because just about all homeowners have insurance that covers roofs, roofing companies can raise the price beyond what it inherently should be because the homeowner doesn't pay the full amount. Moreover, the homeowner feels like he or she is getting a deal because "insurance covers it." Never mind one's premium and the roof's inflated cost.

The same is true of education. If it is assumed that most students will have either scholarships or loans to defray tuition, then tuition can skyrocket without the consequence of losing business. When it feels like nobody can pay—hence the scholarships and loans—the *reality* is that everybody can pay, because they don't see the bill as it truly exists, for the facts of payment are obnubilated and postponed.

Once enough people cover the price of education, home repairs, or medical services with their insurance, those prices irrecoverably inflate until the services are unattainable without insurance. This is the technology or idea that never should have entered the world. And when insurance reaches a sufficiently large clientele, all who remain are forthwith consumed. What is the cutoff for that critical mass? There are two: First, when enough consumers use insurance that the business does not need the patronage of any others (e.g., when universities have enough students with loans that they don't need any self-paying students to fill classrooms); and second, when the insurance is compulsory or somehow mandated. In the case of medical insurance, both have happened.

So, what are the consequences of this regrettable knowledge? Two have been mentioned already; prices go up, and virtually everybody now needs insurance to afford service. But there are even more deleterious side effects than these.

The gravest such affront is that when prices become unaffordable for the average person, the product—in this case, medical care—becomes dictated by insurance. On the patient-facing side, care is directed neither by oneself nor one's medical experts, but the external entity of insurance. Insurance decides where patients can go, what care they receive, the duration it will last, the treatments that can be prescribed, the medicines permitted, and how much an individual will pay for each piece of the puzzle. The sordidness continues on the medical provider's side. Insurance companies have supplanted the knowledge, experience, and good sense of those who actually provide the care. Indeed, the position of caretaker has been usurped from the nurse, doctor, and rest of the team, and it has been assumed by the insurance companies who now orchestrate the proceedings.

Finally, the current system of medical insurance has erected great barriers against even receiving that limited, unconscionable shadow of care. A patient has a better chance of understanding the subtleties of his or her own neurosurgery than the amount it will cost. Enough jargon has entered the world of insurance that soon—like income tax—patients will be forced to hire subject-matter experts to make their payments, just as caretakers have to when submitting the bills themselves. The problem compounds when not even the place-of-treatment itself knows or can determine what a routine procedure will cost, since the insurance system results in a different cost per person per instance, even if the sought-after care remains unchanged. Indeed, the result, uttered thousands of times a day is, "We can't tell you how much it will cost until we bill it."

At the end of the day, it is neither the patient nor the physician, but the insurance company, who is king of healthcare. He has entrenched himself through absolute command of finances on all fronts. He strengthens his bulwarks one brick at a time. With diabolically astute cunning, he attempts to turn the population against each other. His medicine is toxic, not healing, though he offers clever reasoning to the contrary. We, the subjects, must therefore unite around our common goal and dethrone this false king. We can invite him to participate in rebuilding the kingdom, though we must not naively grant him much authority. As he struggles to maintain power, he will employ an arsenal of intimidation, manipulation, and declaration, but we will find our courage through this question: As medical insurance has enlarged, assumed more influence, and played helmsman for the entire system, has medical care become more accessible or less, more affordable or less, more ethical or less, more expedient or less? That is to say, are we better or worse off with it than we were without it?

Wrongful determinants of care

Turning our attention away from insurance, another of

healthcare's opportunities for improvement is its determinants of care. In medicine's pure form, there would be hearty collaboration between the patient's needs and desires, and the caregivers' judgments and abilities. The collaboration would be limited only by resources and the extent of our society's medical knowledge, both of which can be overcome in time. But in the current state, at great frequency, patients' needs are unmet, and their desires are derogated. At the same time, caregivers are hindered from treating based upon their good sense and skill.

Insurance companies are one culprit. Their partners-in-crime—exploitative pharmaceutical companies—are also guilty for similar reasons. Together, they do not ask, but *tell* medical experts how and when to treat their patients, and they do not ask, but *tell* patients what ailments they have and how they will be addressed. These two aside, however, there are at least two other dominating external influences that govern care—lawsuits and legislation.

The threat of lawsuit breathes so forcefully down the neck of everyone who interacts with a patient that very often the chart is treated at the expense of the patient. Whereas a nurse's primary role was once compassionate care, to the great displeasure of all parties involved, it is now charting. Whereas a physician formerly ordered only the tests that were justifiably necessary and reasonably within the patient's best interest, he or she is now compelled to order one of everything and two of most, lest some plaintiff's attorney claim haphazard treatment.

Indeed, there is nothing wrong with either thorough documentation or thorough examination, but there is everything wrong with an unnecessary surfeit due to fear of a civil lawsuit or even criminal indictment. For a future world wherein medical testing has no unintended consequences, resources are not limited, and costs are nonissue, perhaps all people can routinely receive all-encompassing examinations that account for nearly every known condition. That would be a welcome day, but it is not today.

At present, many routine medical tests have nonnegligible risks most easily seen with the mild and moderate radiation that X-rays and CTs respectively emit. The demands upon the resources themselves and the staff who facilitate such tests also stress the system, as ten-hour waits in emergency departments readily evince. Additionally, a balanced approach to medical treatment would consider the monetary cost to the patient and attempt to protect his or her non-medical wellbeing. Compelling patients to undergo unnecessary testing or procedures for the unalloyed sake of hedging against lawsuits is as unethical as not providing treatment that is clearly indicated.

Finally, even more than those who exploit the law for profit, there are those who create the laws to service special interests. What began as reasonable regulations for the sake of protecting those who interact with the healthcare system has swelled into a corpulent barrier to treatment. Though not yet as pervasive as insurance companies, pharmaceutical companies, or unscrupulous attorneys, overzealous regulation quickly stifles whatever progress the other three do not. Perhaps, though, the most condemning action of legislation is that it not only permits the other three to take hold of healthcare but paves their road and diverts all competing traffic.

The unholy syndicate of these four—the *Syndicate*—interwoven and supporting each other, creates most of the barriers to improving our society's healthcare system. In the process of such overt obstructionism, it will be easy to digress toward diatribes and disillusionment, yet it is still more important to remain fixed on the prize—creating a healthcare system that matches our quality as a species.

Prevalence of price gouging

Healthcare is riddled with price gouging. Two power cords can have the same specifications, contain the same materials, and have undergone identical assembly, yet the one that is labeled *hospital-grade* will invariably cost triple its counterpart. Now, it is understandable that many medical items will be expensive, both for the items themselves and the abundant research that went into their development, but these are crucial to the process and would be utilized irrespective of any regulations governing them. For example, few physicians would substitute a claw-peen roofing hammer for a reflex hammer; the latter is a specialized tool. But as we are nigh upon the point of seeing hospital-grade televisions in patient waiting areas, and as the burden it places on the system is no small thing, it is imperative that we reevaluate and ask what ought to be medical grade, how it differs from its non-Aesculapian analog, and if the people making such determinations are the proper authorities.

Less tangible than equipment, but inestimably important, is education. The medical world has suffered the same extreme inflation in education as has been experienced by all other disciplines, the causes of which are not specific to medicine. However, the healthcare system has an additional burden not acutely felt in many other fields; namely that medical education is channeled through Syndicate-sanctioned monopolies. Unpacking this, most people who work in the healthcare system—even those who do not treat or even, necessarily, interact with patients—are required to have some type of certification or license sanctioned by the Syndicate. Furthermore, insurance will refuse to pay for treatment given to a patient who might have, in any way, interacted with non-credentialed personnel. Finally, as it pertains to overpriced education, there is rarely more than a single body that is authorized to bestow the credentials.

Physicians, for example, are rightly proud that they, not lawmakers, legitimize new physicians. In a sense, this is true, for the pipeline of medical education, including its milestone exams, is created and overseen by an organization of physicians. Yet, it is also true that not a single graduate can practice medicine without a license from the state. That license, in turn, is available only to those who fulfill its credentials by having graduated from an approved institution, having passed the requisite examinations, and having ongoing education through the same. In this way, because the educational and licensing pipeline is overseen by a Syndicate-sanctioned monopoly, it is, in fact, the Syndicate—not fellow physicians—who establishes membership in that order.

Not only physicians, but all would-be providers of care have one—or possibly few—means through which they can achieve their ends. Here, we consider paramedics, nurses, dieticians, yoga therapists, and so many others. And when there are so few channels, the process becomes both hellish and costly. What is more, those burdens inevitably fall to the patient.

Finally, it would be remiss to mention the medical system's exorbitant price gouging and not include pharmaceuticals. What balance can be struck between the price of a pill—minuscule but indispensable—and the inordinate quantities of time and money that are invested in its research, development, and production? Is there a regulation or, more preferably, a virtue, that can protect the patient without trammeling the laborious process behind the product? A clever reader knows the solution. Let the rest of us help foster a world in which it can be realized.

Top-down oversight

One of the final difficulties against realizing an adequate or better healthcare system is its partitioned, siloed infrastructure. What has advanced from a handful of broad-scoped, undereducated providers—the physician, the apothecary, the barber-surgeon—has passed through reasonability and into a network of such specialization that neither the provider nor the patient has much sense about where the appropriate treatment can be found. Additionally, once in partnership with the indicated medical provider, there are still barriers between the treatment thereat provided and the treatment from any other medical expert. That is to say that interdisciplinary communication and collaboration are wanting.

Much of the issue is rooted in the Syndicate and the generalized lack of control felt by those who interact with it. Consequently, not only do the monopolies of insurance, education, etc. insist that each facet of care be compartmentalized and separated from all other aspects, but those who see such a system's failings and desire to overcome them are quickly defeated in both mind and business. Not only does patient care diminish and provider efficiency crumble, but these siloes foster an environment of mistrust between providers. Patients, above all others, receive the short end of the stick.

For example, consider the paramedic who, in the field, places an intravenous line in a patient. Upon arrival in the emergency department (ED), the staff then ignores or removes the medic's line and places their own. Then, upon admission to the hospital, that staff ignores or removes the ED line and, again, places *its* own. Across this common series of events, the patient received and was charged for three IV lines when only one was indicated. Each step along the way, the receiving providers did not trust the work of those who cared for the patient last, even though the line's integrity can be quickly and easily verified. The ED staff does not trust that a medic knows to clean the site before injection or that he or she can establish patent access. The floor staff erroneously believes the same about those in the ED. These superfluous steps are danced to the unharmonious tune of lawsuit, for God be with the nurse whose patient develops a complication and is asked by a lawyer, "And tell the court why you did not start *your own* intravenous line on the patient?" Never mind the harm and expense to all other patients.

Thus, we note that one consequence of the Syndicate's top-down oversight is the silo, the narrow container to which one aspect of medical care is confined and separated from all the rest. Another consequence is the previously discussed presence of monopolies and their ability to price gouge all who stumble their way. Even more, there is the unnecessary credentialing, also discussed previously, which, abiding its current course, will soon require the custodial staff to have two years of classroom training, four months of rotations at approved facilities, one thousand-dollar licensing exam, and annual continuing education. And let us not forget the hospital-grade mop bucket.

When the masters sit atop all others and dictate the course of events, the direst consequence is, initially, the most perplexing. For we wonder how a field characterized by highly educated, disproportionately kindhearted individuals can be so grossly mismanaged. Where are the creative solutions? Where is the innovation? The answer is indeed top-down oversight, that the system is overseen not by those who work in the field, but by the Syndicate—insurance, pharmaceuticals, courts, and lawmakers.

The infrastructure established by the Syndicate not only creates the siloes described in this subsection, but it vehemently opposes any breakaway from them. Interdisciplinary cooperation threatens its bases of power and profit. Therefore, the Syndicate creates regulations that prevent specialties from overlapping, prosecutes the providers who treat in that way, and refuses to defray the expenses through insurance. Ax the physician's office that employs an uncredentialed janitor and furnishes his workstation with a non-hospital-grade mop bucket; defrock the physician who deemed it so; condemn the other employees; refuse prescriptions to the patients who seek their care; amerce the medical director and the office manager; and lock in the Bastille any who dare attempt to overcome the will of the Syndicate.

The medical field is replete with creative individuals who understand its problems and who have ideas about how to fix them. Yes, innovation is difficult, but how much more so when it is suppressed by the autocrats managing the industry? Within the Syndicate's parameters, whatever changes can be implemented are small and impotent, both in scope and effect.

Conclusion

There is but one two-part solution that can address the crisis facing our healthcare system—return control from the Syndicate back to its rightful owners, the patients and their providers. And, after having done so, remove the horse blinders it has made us wear, and look to sweeping and holistic changes.

Until then, what intermediary steps can be taken? First and foremost, the focus on medical insurance must change. Not only can we no longer think of it as the only problem and solution, but we need to stop thinking in terms of source (government, private, or mixed), price (paid from wallets, paychecks, or taxes), and scope (none, limited, or all encompassing). Rather, we need to think of insurance as a tool and ask about its purpose and what functions it can manage. We must assert that the healthcare system is more than medical insurance.

We must allow oversight to be lateral—from within the system—rather than top-down, from above.

We must overturn regulation. Let the practices themselves deem what roles require certified education versus on-the-job training, likewise what equipment or skill is appropriate for each given function. Alternatively, the hitherto unregulated or self-regulated giants—the Syndicate—must be regulated, as it has proven itself unfit for the responsibilities it enjoys.

We must disband the monopolies that the Syndicate has created. Competitors must be allowed to rise. New institutions must be formed to educate; new certifying bodies sanctioned to demand excellence and reassure other of the same; new vendors to create technology and medicine; new roles to fill voids and bridge gaps in treatment; new facilities to treat; and new payers to cut and consume costs in the ways that insurance has failed to do. Of course, all of these must be allowed to arise organically and from within. If the Syndicate's crushing hand is removed, we will be astonished at how quickly ingenious solutions will emerge, and we need only keep the hand lifted to watch them flourish.

We must allow for both transparency and simplicity, especially as it applies to a patient's costs. The price for services—say, for a blood test, or for a physical—should be available to the patient in advance of service. As each customer in the grocery store pays the same for the same bag of flour, so too must healthcare price an item by the item, not the patient. In a similar vein, there should be a single bill. A restaurant purveys a single check despite the many hands that create and serve the meal. If it used healthcare's current approach, a diner and his family would receive, throughout the five months following their meal, one bill from the chef, one from the server, one from the restaurant itself, with each bill likely including items that were never ordered and that are priced differently than another's bill from the very same day.

∽

At the outset of this foray into healthcare, the reader was duly warned that no elixir would be offered. The healthcare system is vast and intricate. Moreover, it is daily changing and advancing. The solutions cannot come from a single author, a single book, or a single anything. Healthcare's needs are legion, its challenges daunting. Good thing, then, that there is no shortage of individuals, groups, and organizations with ideas to implement. Presently, those who wish to create change are shackled, but we have identified which jailors hold the keys. Let us then unlock our potential and gift to ourselves and our posterity a better world of healthcare, one that will match our boundless capacity for all that is good.

PART 3

COMMON CONCERNS AND MATTERS OF THE GOVERNMENT

CHAPTER 7
ELECTIONS AND PSEPHOLOGY

> *Pick a leader who will make their citizens proud. One who will stir the hearts of the people, so that the sons and daughters of a given nation strive to emulate their leader's greatness.*
>
> ~Suzy Kassem, from *Rise Up and Salute the Sun*

> *Dictators are not in the business of allowing elections that could remove them from their thrones.*
>
> ~Gene Sharp, from *Dictatorship to Democracy*

Pseudo-psephology: A quick look at electoral systems

The United States electoral system is not the only valid way to choose candidates, cast votes, and determine winners. Though many polities across the world use this same scheme, it is inarguably flawed. Better systems are available, but first, we must understand our own current system whose hallmarks are the following:

1. Each voter has one vote to cast.

2. The candidate who receives the most votes wins the election.

This system is called *winner take all*, or *first past the post* (FPTP) because whichever candidate secures the most votes wins the election regardless of how slim the margin of victory might have been. (The US presidency sounds like an exception because it is determined by winning the majority of electoral votes and not the national popular vote; nevertheless, the Electoral College itself uses FPTP.)

This system is rudimentary and, arguably, better than having no elections at all—but just barely. Children stumble upon FPTP when first learning social skills. In some facets of life, simplicity is golden, but in elections it fails each individual and society as a whole. At a cursory glance, FPTP seems fair, but in practice, its foundational mathematics perforce demands several adverse effects. The most egregious five are the following:

1. Compels a two-party system. Even in a newly formed democracy with abundant political parties, the mathematics that govern FPTP necessitates that, over time, only two parties will remain.

2. Prevents third parties. Once two parties have been established, third parties are hopeless to win majorities, barring exceptional circumstances.

3. Forces strategic voting. Strategic voting requires casting ballots based upon the perceptions of other voters. More plainly, instead of voting for their first choice, voters must choose whoever they think has the best chance of winning, lest the more off-putting candidate win. Such are based on assumptions about the population's general mood, which is heavily influenced by the media.

4. Rewards negative voting. Closely related to effects one and three, a FPTP system leads to votes *against* the disfavored or feared candidate rather than *for* the preferred one.

5. Invites gerrymandering. Geographical districts can be drawn so that pluralities of the population are cast as minorities. This occurs when electoral boundaries intentionally split a large concentration of one party's supporters into districts that overwhelmingly support the opposing party.

FPTP is an anachronism unfit for the present era. It was the best solution of an age in which the idea of democracy was relatively novel. Truly, we are deeply indebted to our Founding Fathers for leaving behind this system. Indeed, we are also much beholden to the first automobile makers, but as we have improved upon *that* design and thereby improved much else, let us also improve upon the first draft of electoral theory.

The proposed alternative is *ranked-choice voting,* also called *single transferable vote,* STV. Its hallmarks are the following:

1. Each voter completes a ranked ballot, numbering candidates in order of preference. A voter does not need to rank every candidate. If there are twenty candidates on the ballot, the voter may rank his or her top three only, or top one. If the desire is to rank all twenty, or nineteen of the twenty, then that's acceptable also.

2. If, when votes are tallied, a winner has not emerged, the candidate who has gathered the fewest votes is dropped from the race. The votes that candidate received are applied to voters' next choices, and the process repeats until a winner has emerged.

This voting system may seem complicated, and while it is more intricate than FPTP, STV is actually rather simple. Even more importantly, it produces none of the five ill effects mentioned above. And as a bonus, the system can be applied to single-winner elections such as a presidential election, or multiple-winner elections such as gerrymandering-free district representatives.

Political parties

Regardless of which electoral system is used, political parties are inevitable. Few Americans love their party, but nearly all are averse to the opposition. This phenomenon is symptomatic of FPTP. So hostile and fear-inducing is our current method, that the name of the other party is an invective not appropriate for polite or civil company.

In a better world—perhaps wherein STV is used—political parties have a more positive role to play. Because STV does not force a two-party system, it gives smaller parties a fighting chance. Because small-party candidates have strong and real possibilities of winning elections, and because ranked voting assures voters that backing such candidates will not equate to wasted votes or worse, votes for the dreaded antithetical party, this design fosters a society in which smaller parties are possible and voters can find parties that align to their views and values.

Currently, in FPTP, we are led by fear and choose the least of two evils; in the better world of STV, we are led by hope and choose our favorite, followed by our second favorite, etc.

Whether we retain the current systems or adopt sensible ones, and whether there are two political parties or many, the nature of parties must be assessed.

First and foremost, a political party is not inherently different from a social club, the distinction is that the former is politically driven and seeks to hold office. It can be as narrow or universal as it desires. One party might strive to appeal to nearly all Americans, hoping to field candidates in all elections ranging from city councils to state senates to the Oval Office. On the other hand, a different party might be focused around a very narrow population within a county district and field candidates for those elections only.

Whether vast or puny, political parties are private—not public. Like any social club, a party has the inherent privilege of choosing its own members, provided, of course, that would-be members are not rejected based on unjust criteria. A functional political party comprises like-minded individuals joining together to effectuate their dreams and visions of society. Hence, each party has the prerogative of rejecting would-be members who do not share the party's mores.

Furthermore, each party has the right to govern itself as it sees fit. If a party desires to nominate candidates at random, then let it. If it desires to have an absurdly complicated system of internal elections to decide on its nominee, it can. Moreover, because each party retains the privilege of governing itself, it runs its own primary elections—if it even chooses to have any. The timing, manner, place, and participants are at the party's discretion. To further treat these points:

1. The timing: Provided that the party is ready to submit its candidates' names to the official election by the deadline that exists, no entity has the right to tell that party how to prepare. If the party determines its nominees two years, two months, or two hours before it must submit the names, what of it? (Note that STV allows for parties to field multiple candidates without the possibility of a split ticket.)

2. The manner: A party can use elections (STV, FPTP, or others), lotteries, executive decisions, astrology, and/or whatever else to determine its nominees and internal procedures.

3. The place: Party meetings, internal elections, and other business can be conducted wherever it chooses. A very small party might communicate with its members via

bulletin board and hold all of its functions in a community center. A nationwide party might establish offices throughout the country and hold internal elections at various times for various locations.

4. The participants: If a party chooses to allow only a board of senior members to vote on its nominee, then that's the party's decision. If it desires that all members be allowed to vote, it can institute that rule. If it holds open elections that extend beyond the party's members and into the rest of the nation, or other countries, even, then it can.

In short, all party business is under the party's own purview and discretion. Neither the government nor other parties can affect its methods. The allowance of such external control is a sure and dastardly way to prevent fair elections and suppress political diversity.

Lead-up to election day

The election itself is out of the parties' control and under the government's. Whereas it was up to each party to determine how fair, accessible, and transparent to make itself, the government has a duty to its citizens to ensure that the election has an abundance of fairness, accessibility, and transparency.

Well before election day, the government shall have set a clear deadline for the submission of nominees, with clear rules determining whatever acceptance criteria might exist. After all nominees have been established, preparatory materials should be created and made easily accessible to all eligible voters. These materials should be published well in advance of the election and include at least the following:

1. Sample ballot

2. Itinerary for the election

3. Where to find each candidate's campaign materials

4. Where to find additional information about the election, including what to bring and where to go

Who should vote?

Few people dismiss the notion that elections ought to be restricted from every human being across the globe to some subset thereof. The difficulty lies in establishing that subset. For our own nation, that subset was once narrowly defined, most notably by gender, skin color, and property. Now these restrictions are gone, but others are in place, such as age, citizenship, felony status, and location.

The goal is to make elections as fair and open as possible, while still keeping them appropriately limited. There is a balance. An infinitely open election is actually quite unfair. To illustrate, it would be wrong for a city to forbid residents over six-feet-tall from voting for city council members; such immoral disenfranchisement is well-understood. However, it would be just as wrong to allow every resident of the state to vote in said city election. People living outside of that city council's jurisdiction have no right to overwhelm the city's own internal proceedings.

There are three factors that inform eligibility:

1. Competence: Are you equipped to vote? Because shaping a society requires more responsibility than even the most precocious six-year-old possesses, no one has yet made a serious claim that six-year-olds should be enfranchised. Lucid adults only should be afforded the privilege of voting. Society determines its definition of adulthood, and it ought to account for attributes such as understanding and responsibility. (See the chapter "Coming of Age" for

more on adulthood and its defining features.)

2. Investment: Will you live under your decision? When people are meaningfully invested in the outcome, they make better decisions. Only those who will be subject to the laws and officials ought to vote upon them. For example, only residents of a certain state may vote in that state's elections. Investment is not only geographic, but temporal. Visitors, vacationers, temporary residents, and all others passing by have no meaningful stake in the election because they will be long gone before its effects are manifest. Therefore, only established residents/citizens of a polity should vote in the elections of those polities. Of course, any qualifier in any regulation is subject to abuse. There is a balance between Jim Crow and a free-for-all. Avoid overcomplication. If a person has had their primary residence in a place for at least twelve months, then they're established.

3. Standing: Have you earned the privilege? Or, more accurately, have you lost it? If competence and investment earn the prerogative of voting, then—provided that those two remain—perhaps only loss of standing can dismiss it. Yet, strong caution is advised before disenfranchising due to standing. This practice lies at the door of vicious discrimination. One can argue that a felon has lost his right to vote because he has demonstrated egregious disregard for the place and its laws, but the slippery slope is that only the virtue of lawmakers—not any diktat binding them—determines what is or is not a felony, what does or does not bar a citizen from good standing. What prevents the outlawing of certain political views? Nothing. Therefore, to protect the right to vote, it ought never be repealed due to standing.

Election Day

Americans' widespread lack of confidence in the electoral process reflects negatively on our nation and its leadership. Election day ought to be a source of pride and patriotism. Even if our first-choice candidate does not win, we should feel content to have participated and satisfied that the results are fair. The current reality is quite different.

Expectations are the first key to satisfaction. Under the current system, expectations are murky, untenable, or outright nonexistent. Given that elections are one of the greatest hallmarks of a free society, election day ought to be orderly and dignified. If the government should make expenditures toward anything, surely this is a top contender. We need to dismiss the haphazard model and implement a system that is accessible, safeguards against fraud, and outlines realizable timelines. To treat each of these:

1. Accessibility begins prior to election day with the distribution of the preparatory materials mentioned above, including information such as where to vote and what the ballot will contain. On the day itself, no voter should have to travel great distances, compete for parking, wait long to cast a ballot, suffer harassment from media or campaigners, encounter biased poll workers, feel pressured or rushed, or endure any other obstacles that make participating in the election a hassle.

2. Safeguarding against fraudulence is a difficult feat, as any process involving such vast numbers of participants and moving parts—compounded with the stakes—is *always* subject to dishonesty. While creating a perfect system is unattainable, there are realistic measures that can be taken. To offer only one solution, if each ballot were

created with a randomized identifier, then each voter could track how his or her ballot was counted, while still maintaining confidentiality. (See below for more details.)

3. The idea of an election *day* is satisfying but impractical. It establishes an expectation that, at the end of one day, all votes should have been tallied and the winner declared. The reality, though, is that one day is simply not enough time to perform a satisfactory job. Instead, the expectation should be that a winner will *not* be determined until two, three, or even four days after the vote. People can live with that, even if it's on the edge of their seats.

Vignette of a better world

Consider the following scenario for an accessible, fraud-forfending, expectation-managing election day:

Well over a month ago, you received your preparatory materials, part of which informed you where to go and what the election's timeline would be. Conveniently located from your permanent address, a large space has either been rented or volunteered. It will certainly be large enough to accommodate voters throughout the day, even at peak times. No one will have to wait long to participate.

After waiting in line for about five minutes, an amicable poll worker checks you in. She examines your identification and crosses your name off a list of that location's voters. Your preparatory materials informed you of how to easily request a different location, but this one was the most agreeable anyway. You are invited to fill out your ballot via tablet or paper. Electronic votes are tabulated quicker, but since the election results won't be determined for another three days, paper will not cause any problems.

You choose the tablet. The ballot has clear directions and an intuitive design. You rank your candidates, review your choices, and confirm your submission. The last step is acknowledging the printout you've just received. It is a copy of your ballot and has a randomized identifier. Time to review it for accuracy. If there were a mistake, you would wave over a poll worker skilled in resolving the issue. No voter should ever leave the polling location until they are satisfied that their ballot has been received accurately. But since your printout receipt was accurate, you click submit and officially cast your vote. You exit the polling place, anonymized receipt in hand, and notice that those who cast paper ballots have carbon copies of their submissions. From start to finish, the process took fewer than twenty minutes.

But the election process is not over yet, as the itinerary you received in your preparatory materials informs you. To accommodate people of every schedule, the polls opened Tuesday morning at 12:00 a.m. and will remain open until midnight. Because voting is so important, after the polls close, workers will organize and tabulate through the night so that, by 9 a.m. sharp the following day the ballots will be published.

Voters are encouraged to review the results, which are posted online and at every polling location. The ballots, of course, lack any identifying information except for their randomly assigned identifier. Using that identifier, you locate your recorded ballot and ensure that it exactly matches your receipt. You have until 11:59 p.m.—and not a minute later—to submit a challenge to your ballot.

Submitting a challenge is as easy as walking into your polling location and informing workers that your ballot was miscounted. Your receipt is your proof. Without the receipt, you cannot challenge; with it, your challenge cannot be ignored. The existence of your challenge—though not you or your information—is made public for transparency's sake. Anyone can look online or at a polling location to see what challenges exist, and with receipts, each person can confirm the accuracy of his or her own ballot. Lastly, at noon on Friday, the results are published.

Eighty-four ample hours were allowed for this important process, but that extended period of time didn't cause you to doubt it. You knew that—regardless of how quickly votes were cast and tabulated, or even if there were not a single challenge—results would not be published a moment sooner than noon Friday. In fact, it was far better than thinking the election was over at 6 p.m. Tuesday, only to realize that the media tried to declare the winner before a vast swath of the citizenry had even voted.

Additionally, you feel confident that your vote was counted accurately, and that only honestly cast ballots were accepted. You knew your polling location and how many people were assigned there. You witnessed your attendance being recorded and know that no one tried to steal your place. That would have been difficult anyway, considering that you brought your photo ID. It was easy to verify that your ballot was counted accurately, and you were reassured by the voter-friendly challenge process that, if something had been messed up along the way, it would have been resolved.

With such transparency, you can determine the election results yourself if you have the time and some light programming skills. (The author has created such an example at github.com/LeBoot/Practical-Advice-for-a-Better-World.) By knowing how many voters were assigned to each location, and by being able to see the ballots online, you could validate that no polling location recorded more votes than its assigned number of voters. Because challenges are publicly indicated, you could also see if any challenges existed, knowing that each voter can confirm their own challenge status.

Friday's noontime announcement is bittersweet: Your first choice did not win. Under the old system you would have been furious. Technically, your employer had the duty to let you miss work so that you could cast your ballot, but as an hourly worker, you really didn't want to. You wish you could have gone before or after work, but with twelve-hour shifts, it just wasn't feasible. You spent your lunch break driving across town, close to home where your polling location was. You wish you could have requested the one across the street from your work, but no such process exists—or, maybe it does, but you can't seem to find any information about these things.

Anyway, after waiting in line for what felt like an hour, you finally filled out your ballot. With all the horror stories of ballots being unreadable to the tabulator, you wondered if yours will even be counted—or worse, counted for the other guy—Team Orange. His presidency will be your worst nightmare. You love the third-party candidate you campaigned for. She was Team Purple's nominee and sounded like a fresh start for the country. You think that most American's support her, but now, it's game time and you know that team Purple doesn't stand a chance. As good as she is, she can't be allowed to split Team Yellow's vote, as Team Yellow is the only hope of preventing Team Orange from sitting at the Big Chair, so you held your nose as you reluctantly cast your ballot for Yellow—at least he's not Orange.

You didn't have time for lunch today, and the rest of your shift was punishing because of it, but finally you're home. You turn on the news to hear that Team Yellow is leading by a huge margin—woo-hoo!—it should be finalized in an hour or two, but since there's work tomorrow, you go to bed.

Waking up the next morning, you are surprised to hear that Team Orange is now leading. Apparently, tens of thousands of votes from swing districts have finally been counted. You hear many explanations for how this happened, but none of them quite sit right. You wonder if it's even statistically plausible that the ballots are arriving the way they're being reported. You wish you could see what the fate of your own ballot was, but even if you could, what would you do? Sign an affidavit for one of Team Yellow's inevitable lawsuits? Not likely. So, you return to your day-to-day resentful of the system and confident that something deliberate and nefarious happened with the *real* outcome of the election. It's doubtful that you will ever participate again. It's almost like the process was designed to make you give up. Such is the habit of a no-win system.

But how glorious that those days have passed! Here's what really happened, now that we are living in a better world with a better electoral system: Friday's noontime announcement is still bittersweet. Your first choice did not win; in fact, neither your first nor second choice was elected, but your third choice—still high on your list—won. Your first choice was a niche candidate with a low chance of winning, but, with the ranked ballot of an STV system, you were confident supporting him, knowing that if he didn't win, your vote would pass to your second choice. Your second choice was strong; she and your third choice were from the same party, but both were in the election because there was no fear of a split vote. Many of her supporters did like you and ranked your third choice as the next best. This year, you cast your vote on your way to work, no matter that it was 5 a.m. Your polling location had 450 voters assigned. You see that 425 ballots were cast. Only two ballots were challenged, and both were resolved, and voter confirmed. Third choice is still good, and—more importantly—you are confident that the election was fair.

CHAPTER 8

MEANS OF GOVERNANCE

> *If one set of private subjects may at any time take upon themselves to punish another set of private subjects just when they please, it's such a sort of government as I never heard of before; and according to my poor notion of government, this is one of the principal things which government is designed to prevent; and I own I had rather be a slave under one master (for I know who he is I may perhaps be able to please him) than a slave to a hundred or more whom I don't know where to find, nor what they will expect of me.*
>
> ~Theophilus Lillie

> *I consider the foundation of the Constitution as laid on this ground: that "all powers not delegated to the United States, by the Constitution, nor prohibited by it to the states, are reserved to the states or to the people." To take a single step beyond the boundaries thus specially drawn around the powers of Congress, is to take possession of a boundless field of power, not longer susceptible of any definition.*
>
> ~Thomas Jefferson

What is government?

Backdropping each controversial issue that wrests the fibers of society is a philosophical question about the powers that govern. One viewpoint fundamentally leans toward legislation while the other leans away from it. Failure to acknowledge and reconcile this difference impedes meaningful progress and creates bitter divisions.

To use a contemporary topic as an example: Suppose that we seek to reduce vehicle emissions. One proposal is to ratify legislation that punishes people associated with higher-emission vehicles and rewards people associated with lower-emission vehicles. This is the law-based solution. The other proposal is for those who believe in the cause to adopt lower-emission vehicles, support companies that pursue technology to the same, and attempt to educate the ignorant and sway the skeptical. This solution avoids legislative action.

Despite a common end goal of reduced vehicle emissions, these approaches are not easily syncretized because they are intrinsically disparate. Beneath the outward expression of vehicle emissions, there is a more foundational belief that asks, *what is government?*

Taking a reductive approach, we can aver that government is a formal system that attempts to stabilize societal groups.

Skipping over millennia of human history, there seem to be two broad philosophies, herein referred to as *overseers* and *guardians*. These appellations are similar because both are rooted in protection. Before diving any farther, it must be stressed that these philosophies transcend, and are wholly separate from, the mindsets described as "conservative" or "liberal" and their associated political parties. Overseers and guardians exist across the entire political spectrum and even apolitical realms.

Overseers use government to protect outcomes, whereas guardians use government to protect self-determination.

Overseers believe that government legislation should guide people's actions toward certain end goals. Guardians believe that government should protect individuals' power—that is, liberty—to determine their own fates. Finally, overseers believe that the government has a duty to steer people away from, or altogether forbid, self-detrimental behaviors. Guardians, however, believe that the government should allow people to choose their own courses, even if self-detrimental—provided that such courses do not cause immediate harm to others.

Another example: Overseers tend toward helmet laws, believing that government has the responsibility to ensure others' safety, even if the concern is no more noble than wanting to avoid these people's hospital bills. Guardians believe that government lacks the inherent authority to force a person to wear a helmet, that taking such a risk is part of one's sovereign prerogatives. It is not that overseers care about safety and guardians do not. Rather, the underlying issue boils down to this: Does government mandate others to behave as it prefers, or does government safeguard self-determination?

It is the timeless question of what love requires. Does love step back, even when painful? When do parents begin letting their children make their own decisions, perhaps erring along the way? Overseers view humanity as children and government as a protective parent—perhaps adjudicating against the children's will, but justified by reasoning that parents are wiser than children. Guardians view humanity as adults and government as other adults who can guide and advise, but who have no authority to force, even to avoid detriment.

The overseers and guardians' philosophies can easily appear as only preferential differences, of which there is no objective right or wrong. With so many people of either opinion, the debate seems like a Red Team verses Blue Team argument in which neither is intrinsically superior. Beling first impressions, however, there *is* a correct answer, though aside from moral arguments, the superior philosophy does not outshine the other of its own right, necessarily, but because its alternative is fundamentally flawed.

The overseer viewpoint has three salient shortcomings:

First, protecting outcomes assumes that certain outcomes are better than others. While, of course, this is often the case, the targeted outcomes are, nevertheless, opinions. Inviolable laws of God and Nature do not outline the chosen courses of action. They are human estimations formed by imperfect people from imperfect evidence, imperfect understanding, and many other imperfections. In short, there is no guarantee that the proposed outcomes are desirous, and there is far less certainty that the means of achieving those outcomes is appropriate or will bring us to the end goal.

Further evidence of these uncertainties lies in the population's divided opinions. If a truth or course of action was manifest, then there would be widespread acknowledgment of the same, resulting in support for that common goal. For so many critical issues, though, there is a nearly even split; this evinces the fact that either or both of the proposed outcomes and proposed roadmaps are dubious.

Second, as the overseer approach to government forces the opinions of some onto the whole, it must be either sinister or cynical. It is sinister if it forces people fully knowing that, if equally informed, they would choose a different course of action. It is cynical if believes that people are either too gormless to understand the proposed courses of action, or not worth the effort to convince.

Third. The most severe flaw of the overseer attitude is that it grants authority that only feels reasonable if given to friends; if given to enemies, it feels unconscionable. In short, we need to ask each other, "If your opposition were in office, would you still want the government to have these proposed powers?" Overseers enjoy empowering likeminded people; they raise them up, bestow broad powers, and enjoy watching noncompliers pressed into submission. But think, overseer, about what would happen if another—who does not share your opinions—were to rise and replace your master? "Woe is me," will be your cry.

The nature of the world is *change*. The people who hold power today will not hold it in the future. Therefore, every member of society must exercise caution when relinquishing liberties, even to someone with similar views. Upon inauguration of the next leader, there might be cause for regret. The overseer philosophy is akin to an absolute, but benevolent, monarch. Give such a monarch—or president, governor, prime minister, Congress, mayor, etc.—undiminished rule, and the world might very well benefit from it. But monarchs die and politicians leave office; those who arise after them are rarely equals.

To assuage the tumult of different parties rising, falling, and leaving great upsets in their wakes, we must not grant such unrestrained powers, even to people we strongly support. The higher road and the more expedient one in the long-term is to limit powers to the point that we can feel comfortable even if an opposing party takes the helm.

The guardian philosophy, then, because of its stability and leniency, is the superior approach to government. Strong opinions and desires to reshape society—as expressed by both camps—are not wrong, but ends do not justify means. As we heartily acknowledge that one race does not have the prerogative of subjugating other races, so too must we come to realize that one political opinion does not have the prerogative of subjugating all others. They can glom legal powers and create laws that legitimize their actions, but that does not make the actions defensible, nor exculpate those responsible.

Understanding the differences between the guardian and overseer philosophies allows us to work toward realistic solutions. It helps explain why intelligent people often can't agree on how to achieve common goals, for if one person wants to force others but the second refuses that route, then there is no path forward. These same differences guide opinions about governance and its means. Guardians value limitations of power and do not view the law as a tool for reshaping others. In their minds, laws are largely limited to restricting the government itself, safeguarding self-determination, and protecting people's immediate lives, livelihoods, and liberties.

Interactions between the government and itself

All organizations owe it to themselves and their success to conduct periodic, if not continuous, internal reassessments. As even the most well-kept house accumulates dust, as even the best pathfinders stray and need to retake their positions, so too must organizations undergo maintenance. The government at all levels must look in the mirror and ask how it has strayed from its purpose, what vestigial structures it unnecessarily conserves or even asseverates, and which pieces of the whole create more friction than they're worth. In short, it's time for spring cleaning.

The Tenth Amendment to the US Constitution declares that, "The powers not delegated to the United States by the Constitution, nor prohibited by it to the States, are reserved to the States respectively, or to the people." Many countries, of course, have no such specific restrictions to federal power, and in reality, the United States itself no longer does. The broad language of the Tenth Amendment, which is meant to be its strength, has been subjected to legal trickery until, now, this once-powerful protection has been brought low and enervated.

The Constitution does, in fact, reserve certain powers for the very highest level of government—powers such as declaring war and coining money. With enough sophistry and dishonest reasoning, however, anything and everything can be subsumed by the relatively few bailiwicks overseen by the federal government. And, in the nearly two-dozen decades since the Tenth Amendment's ratification, nearly everything has.

Good companies frame decisions by their mission statements and values, the faithful constantly return to their creeds, and successful individuals write their goals and remind themselves daily of them. Using these practices as examples, the government must return to its own missions, values, creeds, and goals, which, though not written as such, are manifest in any of its founding documents, including the ill-treated Constitution (1788) and Bill of Rights (the first ten amendments, 1791). There must be realignment to these purposes.

In the process, the oft-overlooked Tenth Amendment needs to be reaffirmed, defiladed, and strengthened. The existing amendment should not itself be updated; rather, new clarifying laws should be added. As the government's current practice is to do whatever is not expressly forbidden, or to do what is expressly forbidden under the pretense of an enumerated power, we must redefine its scope of authority.

In a legal analogy, the burden of proof *should* be on the prosecution, not the defendant. In other words, the person who wants to accuse you of a crime must prove that you committed it, rather than make you prove that you did not. In some cases, this is true, but in many cases it—unjustly—is not. For example, the Internal Revenue Service makes you prove that you gave the charitable deduction you claimed, rather than providing proof to the contrary.

Using this language, the government ought to bear the *burden of proof* for the authority of its proposed laws and implementations. Currently, it tells the people that we must prove its lack of authority. Instead, it should have to expound its clear and undeniable authority—mind you, not through use of legal hokum, but through presentation of explicitly manifest authorization. Indeed, the government must positively prove that it has authority to do something before it acts.

Next, we look to leadership. As many successful churches crumble when their senior pastors leave, and as one influential executive's retirement can cause a cascade failure throughout a prosperous company, leadership must be renewed often lest one person be responsible for keeping the whole ship afloat. Knowing that the nascent United States needed to find a way to succeed outside of only himself, George Washington had the prescience to leave the presidency after two terms.

Since all humans are mortal, any leader who occupies too much time in office necessarily sets his or her dominion on the course of failure. As mentioned above, if one pastor is the only preacher, or if one executive is a company's only personality, then those organizations are doomed. Even if those leaders, while inaugurated, are exemplary, they cannot maintain their positions forever. As such, ensuring long-term prosperity is necessarily more important than short-term success. History has shown that a country that thrives under a great king can, after his death, quickly wither as one less suited assumes the throne.

Term limits are the solution to this dilemma. Four-term President Franklin D. Roosevelt proved that a two-term precedent cannot check a man of power. That lesson learned, the country ratified the Twenty-Second Amendment limiting the presidency to two terms. Notwithstanding, what about those who do not hold that single highest office in the land? What about the people who spend the better part of a lifetime—three, four, or more decades—in Congress and other seats of government?

Some might retort, "If you don't want those people in office, then vote them out!" However, as discussed in the chapter "Elections and Psephology" the two-party system that inevitably results from the world's most popular voting system essentially prevents meaningful turnover in government. In polities that lean decisively toward one party, that party's candidate will remain in office election after election, decade after decade.

The overall suitability and worth of career politicians, after a brief moment of nausea, should make all voters leap upon term limits. Even if one's district was represented by noble George Washington or some other sainted individual, long-lasting success pleads that new leaders be installed regularly. A captain who goes down with his ship is laudable, but a ship that goes down with its captain is an abomination.

Therefore, all elected offices, from city council and mayor to Congress and the presidency, must be subjected to term limits that are appropriate for the offices and their electoral cycles. We must be cautious enough to err on the side of shorter tenure, and we must be disciplined enough to refuse exceptions even for people we like.

In addressing internal means of governance, the final proposal is that legislative bodies adopt the same voting practices argued for in the chapter relevant to that topic. Instead of a *first past the post* (FPTP) system, a *single transferable vote* (STV)—or something similar—should be adopted, in which every voter ranks choices by preference.

In the same way that STV helps the citizenry elect politicians who are preferable, rather than the ones who are least awful, so too can it help our representatives pursue more-agreeable changes—less subjected to backroom negotiations, earmarked bills, and other corrupt practices.

For example, let us return to the proposal of reducing vehicle emissions. Just like FPTP results in a ballot containing two polarizing undesirables, it also gives legislators only two undesirable options for proposed changes. The vote might look like this: Option A, do nothing; Option B, impose harsh standards and punishments.

Suppose that you support reducing emissions but don't agree with punishing people who don't get a new vehicle right away, or you believe that the overall effort is well-intentioned but the practicality of recreating an entire industry overnight is untenable. What do you do? Vote for Option A, and make zero progress whatsoever, or vote for Option B and encourage totalitarianism? Neither extreme is sensible. You have one vote to give, and no one will ask about your reasons for the choice.

Should medical marijuana be legal, yes or no? Yes, because it has several medicinal benefits. But no, because then it will be controlled by insurance, pharmaceutical giants, and the rest of the Syndicate. What if, medicine aside—marijuana aside—you don't think that the government should be allowed to tell you what you can or can't consume. Voting to legalize medical marijuana makes it available to those who need it but subjects it to government boondoggling. Voting against legalization denies it to those who need it and unintentionally sides with those who want to dictate other people's habits. Neither option improves the situation nor captures your view of the matter.

Is it any wonder that so many potential voters are disillusioned and don't even bother to participate?

But imagine a Congress in which several options are proposed. Options A and B are still there, but now there are others:

A. Do nothing.

B. Impose harsh new emissions standards and criminal penalties.

C. Impose new standards for manufacturers but, to offset their financial burdens, allow several years of tax exemption.

D. Update standards for new vehicles, but let existing vehicles run their natural course of degradation and obsolescence.

E. Convert government fleets but let the will of the people guide the outcomes of private business.

F. Focus efforts elsewhere in infrastructure—railways, pedestrian causeways, decentralized production—whose improvements might naturally reshape transportation and, in the process, reduce emissions all the same.

G. Any of the ingenious and fair solutions that many readers of this book no doubt have.

In the absence of binary extremism, this ballot has potential to create meaningful change. The votes are cast, the results tallied, and unsurprisingly, neither A nor B is adopted. There is a brighter future ahead.

∼

Of the countless improvements that can be made regarding the government's internal interactions with itself, these three were just presented:

1. **Positive proof.** Make the government offer irrefragable proof of its authority for its decisions. Erect new barriers, and strengthen existing ones, to prevent it from assuming abilities that it should not have.

2. **Term limits.** All elected offices, regardless of branch or sphere of government, should be subjected to conservative term limits.

3. **Adopt STV.** Internal votes of the government should use a voting system that allows the ranking of many options.

Interactions between the government and its people

Given most circumstances, a person is free to patronize his or her preferred institutions. In those cases, businesses strive to offer something better than their competitors—better qualities, prices, experiences, values, etc. Suppose, then, that a business—say, a hardware store—has poor customer service, an unnavigable website, no return policy, inconvenient hours, unintelligible pricing, ersatz products, and accepts only a single form of payment. That store would be out of business in a week if it didn't make improvements.

On the other hand, imagine a world in which each person is legally required to buy a hammer and screwdriver twice a year. Imagine also that it is illegal for any other business to offer these items. That store would have no incentive to improve its model, nor any repercussions if it didn't. Every law-abiding person would be obliged to patronize the insensate store and tolerate its laughable ineptitude.

This fictitious hardware store is, of course, a metaphor describing the government and its sanctioned monopolies, such as utility companies. What follows is not an argument against these monopolies, nor a consideration of their pros and cons. But since such monopolies exist, their processes must be readdressed. Currently, the government tells the people, "You get what you get." Rather than repine our fates and stomp feet while waiting in line at the Department of Motor Vehicles, let us consider how the government and its people might interact in a better world.

The most salient issue is access. The government should be helpful and inviting, not useless and rude. Granted, although many of the employees at these monopolies, including the customer-facing ones, are warm individuals, the *company* designs its processes in ways that belie their kindness, lead to employee burnout, and create mind-numbing frustration for customers.

To facilitate its services to the people, each level of government should offer a single, central location at which all services are available at convenient times. Ideally, federal and state levels of government would partner with each county or city to adject their own facilities. Additionally, this concept does not preclude satellite locations.

In essence, each state, for example, would have at least one central building or complex at which all of its various departments and services are customer-facing. A state capital complex is a sensible start. At that place—call it the *omphalos of polity*, or OP—people are directed to the offices of whichever departments are needed. And then, most importantly, after walking through *those* doors, help and answers are received. Every interaction a person needs with the state government can be accomplished there; no driving to a different location, no *in person service not available,* nor any such inadequate service. Size and security add difficulty to the OP proposal but consider that the entirety of the government need not be housed there, only what is minimally required to fulfill the needs of face-to-face interactions.

The next iteration of this concept is for state and federal offices to annex additional offices to each local government's OP. At such a place, a person can conduct all government business— those pertaining to local, state, and federal—in a single location. There, he or she can pay city taxes, get information about the city's parks and recreation department, renew state vehicle registration, sign a petition to repeal a state law, apply for federal benefits, and reserve a campsite at a national park.

Imagine a person doing all these things—and so much more— at a single location. Imagine also that its hours of operation were not a subset to the average person's work schedule, but accessible: open 5 a.m. to 10 p.m., six days a week or better. If a grocery store, which values its customers, can organize the personnel to make it happen, then why can't the government?

Continuing with issues of accessibility, each level of government ought to create a single website that mirrors the OP approach. Beginning from a single, appropriately named homepage, the populous should be able to reach their targets with just a few organized clicks.

Such a *virtual omphalos of polity*, VOP, is, admittedly, perhaps a more challenging undertaking than even its brick-and-mortar counterpart. The proper organization, analytics, architecture, maintenance, and adaptability of this great government panoply will require exceptional minds and talent, but this moonshot is not beyond realization whatsoever. If freed from the bureaucracy and red tape that encumber private and public sectors alike, forty sedulous workers could have it up and running within forty months. The head of state who tackles this organizational masterwork can have the project completed before the next election.

Since this VOP is within grasp, let us not limit its utility. Granted it would be an exemplary achievement for an administration to undertake and complete an all-in-one online resource for renewing documents, applying for services, paying bills, etc., but what if, in addition to being a functional resource, it became an intellectual one also? The website could be a resource for learning about the government and what it does.

Imagine access to maps, chains of command, explanations of secretariats, and milestone documents. One of the most important collections would be called *laws and policies*—LP. The LP resource would contain an exhaustive, organized enumeration of all laws, statutes, ordinances, torts, executive orders, policies, precedents, etc.—herein referred to collectively as *edicts*—that have jurisdiction within the VOP's territory. (Given the legion of edicts that exist, it is recommended to reevaluate and reduce the national corpus as described in the chapter "Justice and Jurisprudence." Be warned, though, that this effort is likely a far greater challenge than the OP and VOP together.)

Notwithstanding, because the website and its physical equivalent are the paladins of an accessible government and informed citizenry, and to encourage transparency from elected officials, it is imperative that proposed and new edicts be visibly promulgated. In person, this might look like pamphlets placed throughout the OP listing the newest edicts. Online, it might be a homepage banner linked to a filterable list. This constantly updating list should contain each edict's unabridged text *and* a summary in plain language, also its effective date and the individuals who voted for or signed it. Since lives are bound by these rules, people have the right to know at least that much.

Although real and virtual omphali are monumental achievements toward improving relations between government and its people, they are still inaccessible to a sizable portion of the citizenry. Therefore, the government's duty is to create phone and mail services. Each OP should have a 24/7 call center that can both fulfill requests or forward to whichever OP office is needed.

Furthermore, whether initiated via internet, phone, on-site, or some other means, a person ought to be able to request any documents and receive them, through a preferred channel, free of charge. If forms are required for an application, one should be able to call, be told which forms are needed, request that they be mailed or emailed, and then receive them. Being told that they must be retrieved in person, or even online, is simply unacceptable.

People have the right to access their government, especially as it mandates the use of its services. Because, at least in theory, the government serves at the pleasure of the citizenry, it must make exaggerated efforts to accommodate all within its dominion. Therefore, if something needs to be mailed, it should be mailed quickly and gratis. If you are somewhere in person, it should be there for you. Whether you require a single form or simply want a hardcopy of the entire corpus of edicts, it does not matter. These are, after all, yours.

Finally, because interactions with the government and its monopolies are compulsory, the issue of third-party services needs to be raised. Though the chapter "Consumer Rights" treats third-party services in more detail, herein are a few brief notes on the subject as it relates to government are addressed:

Keeping in mind that, in this context, a *third party* is an entity other than you and the government, such as a bank, payment processor, photographer, or data warehouse company. No government interaction should necessitate the use of third-party services, nor cause undo inconvenience to those who choose not to use them.

A single example can explain this concerning phenomenon: Consider the IRS, which now accepts most tax returns and payments electronically. However, suppose that you want to pay in cash. As of the writing of this book, there are two options:

The first option is to use a third-party payment website that verifies your information then emails printable instructions and a payment code for you to take to a retail chain outlet which accepts no more than $500 per payment, two payments per day, and charges a fee for each transaction. The other choice is to, thirty to sixty days prior to when you want to pay (per IRS recommendation), call the IRS to schedule a one-to-two-hour appointment at a cash-accepting Taxpayer Assistance Center, arrive at the appointed time, and pay. This option is subject to limited availability resulting from pandemics, administrative issues, etc.

The IRS requires that all citizens with income (earned domestic or abroad) and all people earning income inside the country (citizen or not) help it tax them, yet it will not accept the country's own currency except after excessive hardship. Never mind that written on those banknotes, ironically enough, are the words *this note is legal tender for all debts, public and private.* For the organization that demands a hefty fraction of your painfully scant bank interest, the very least it can do is allow you to show up unannounced and surrender your hardscrabble earnings without hassle.

Yet this is not the case. Granted, it *is* easier if you don't pay in cash, but consider: What if you don't have a credit card, perhaps not wanting the ability to burden yourself so easily with debt? And what if you don't have checks to mail because your bank, like most, charges you for ordering them? Or what if you don't have a bank account because maintaining the minimum balance is quite difficult? What if you choose not to use the internet because nearly every free browser is only free because it sells your personal information, and this is the same reason you don't have an email from which to receive your pay-in-cash instructions and code? What if it is not these reasons, but thinking about an elderly relative who has no internet? What if you can't access your bank account because it is held in your maiden name and they won't accept proof of your new one? What if you are skeptical of online payments because, through that very means, you were the victim of identity theft? What if making an appointment sixty days out is simply unfeasible because you receive your schedule weekly and don't have the luxury of time off that the government assumes you do?

Due to pragmatism, ethics, means, situation, stubbornness, and myriad other reasons, what if a person just wants to pay his or her taxes in cash and be done with it? No such luck. Not only the IRS, but most government services depend on third parties and require that you do the same. Since these services are compulsory, such a requirement is unconscionably unjust. There need to be choices that involve no other entities than you and the government, the inconvenience of which is not the cruel and unusual punishment just described. Though third parties ought not be forbidden, they cannot be the only reasonable option.

Furthermore, it must be noted that the government is not a business in the pure sense. Sound practices, including those pertaining to fiscal competence, are not to be ignored, but the government must be bound by higher ideals than profit, or even viability. The government does not have the convenience of outsourcing its business to third parties because it is cheaper than maintaining its own processes. Such outsourcing means that the government has exchanged privacy for money, reducing expenses by giving citizen information to others. But the right to privacy is worth the expense, as is the cause of making the people's government accessible to the people.

~

Of interactions between the government and its people, several improvements were discussed:

1. **Real and virtual omphali of polity.** Each level of government should establish at least one central location at which all services and information can be conveniently enjoyed. There must also be an accompanying online platform to the same effect.

2. **Accessible information.** Forms, documents, and other resources should be available through several channels—in person, online, mail—at no cost whatsoever.

3. **Independence from third parties.** All government services should be accessible without needing to participate in a third-party service nor endure hardships for that choice.

Conclusion

Asking about the means of governance is as grand as asking how one ought to live life. The subject matter is too broad, too circumstantial. We can narrow the focus and ask about only family life, but even at the outset of tackling that titan, we are confronted with the disparities between generalized, philosophical answers, and those whose natures are more specific and actionable. However, acknowledgment of the unconquerable vastness of the subject matter neither precludes the utility of discussion nor excuses avoidance of the same. Therefore, understanding the inexhaustive and reductive limitations just outlined, we assert that means of governance are first approached by asking about the purpose of governance and the governments that will implement those means.

Of all the possible political divisions (conservative vs liberal, pro-X, anti-Y, etc.), this chapter proposed that, beneath all of those, the fundamental divide revolves around a question of protection. Should ascendancies protect outcomes or safeguard self-determination? Those who support protecting outcomes—herein called *overseers*—believe that ends justify means and that laws are tools to reshape the behavior of others. Those who support the protection of self-determination—herein called *guardians*—believe that means supersede ends and that laws are tools for protecting others, not compelling them. Although the superiority of one over the other might seem dubious, guardianship is, in fact, better, as was defended on both moral and pragmatic grounds.

Belief that government is designed not for its own sake but for the people's benefit naturally begets the conviction that its inner workings ought to be designed to protect against corruption, oppression, and poor decisions. Furthermore, guardianship implies that the government ought to be accessible and transparent to its people. Because it only exists for the citizenry, it must exaggerate its efforts to be conveniently available to the people it is designed to serve.

At present, the government elevates itself as a self-important, recondite master—an ascendant panjandrum to whom the commonfolk must dutifully demur, defer, and make displays of reverence and fear. It makes us go to it, humiliating the populous to assert its dominance. It legislates for its own convenience. It makes decisions in the dark and denies the need for either explanation or justification. It answers to no one because it has methodically beaten its master—the people—into obedient submission.

Power is a temptation that easily gives way to corruption, but its dangers are averted by strict limitations and disciplined citizens who value those limitations more than convenience. It is commonly remarked that great tyrants of history have risen to power and committed their despotic crimes through legal channels. All that stands between people's rule over the government and its rule over them is a momentary lapse of vigilance and a few seemingly minor concessions during extraordinary times.

Government is not inherently bad; in fact, the opposite is true. Nevertheless, we have the arduous task of making that unrealized truth a reality. In a better world, the government would be content to protect, organize, and facilitate a noble society free from anarchy and might-makes-right *kratocracy*. In that place, the means of governance will be honest, fair, accessible, and—above all else—focused on serving its people.

CHAPTER 9
TAXATION

> When the income tax came along in 1913, it was as though the country was coming apart at the seams. "It means 100,000 spies to snoop into everybody's business and affairs."
>
> ~David McCullough, from *The Great Bridge*, quoting John Roebling.

> I contend that for a nation to try to tax itself into prosperity is like a man standing in a bucket and trying to lift himself up by the handle.
>
> ~Winston Churchill

Fees for services

Governments need funding. Of its many revenue sources, two are particularly discussion worthy, for they affect the daily lives of every resident: fees and taxes.

Fees accompany nearly every government service. Here, we are not discussing punitive fines, such as those incurred after committing misdemeanors; rather, fees are paid when interacting with government agencies. Consider that official documents such as passports, birth certificates, marriage licenses, driver licenses, construction permits, deeds, etc. are all obtained and filed for nonnegligible fees.

There is no inherent injustice concerning such fees. In fact, one might consider them quite fair, for not all citizens marry nor travel abroad, so perhaps those who do ought to pay for their own marriage licenses and passports without supplementation by those who do not. On the other hand, there is a valid view that fundamental services should not be subjected to nickel-and-dime treatment, that living in the country and paying taxes entitles citizens to certain benefits, such as the ability to obtain basic documents, without fees because the fees have already been included in taxes.

In the private sector, good businesses either pass itemized costs to their consumers, or they include them in the price. Good businesses do not do both. Universal disdain follows a health club that charges for every class and activity on top of hefty monthly membership. It would be worse still if that gym had long lines, unrealistic hours, nonexistent customer service, and monopoly status. And yet, this is exactly how the government treats its citizens, taxing at unconscionably high rates, charging ample fees for all services rendered, and failing to meet even the most basic standards of accessibility and customer service.

Notwithstanding, the fact remains that the government must be funded somehow. The apropos question is not "Why are there fees and taxes?" but rather, "Why both?" In the analogy of the health club, one should be charged either for membership (taxes) or for particular services (fees), but not both, and certainly not at high rates for each.

Muddled mulcting: the jumble of taxes

Fees are a simple matter. One can—or, rather, should be able to—pay for government services via the many techniques that are used with every other transaction of the modern world. Taxes, however, are an altogether different beast. More appropriately, though, one might call it a menagerie, for taxes are not a single entity, but many. Though far too diverse to enumerate exhaustively, to name only a few, there are taxes for income, land, vehicles, businesses, estates, gains, gifts, purchases, and compulsory programs such as healthcare (Medicare) and superannuation (Social Security).

The protean and multifarious nature of taxes notwithstanding, the diversity of taxes becomes a smaller issue when compared to the greater injustice of the current system—given such a substantial number of taxes, the average person has sparsely anything to show for it. At the earning threshold of lower middle income, one can easily lose over half of his or her income to the various taxes just mentioned. Furthermore, such individuals or families who are at the burgeoning cusp of self-support have also, simultaneously, disqualified themselves for many of the aids that their taxes fund.

To compound the abuse, under the current design of income brackets, the earner takes home a smaller percentage of each marginal dollar that he or she earns. The concept of higher incomes being taxed at higher rates diminishes motivation to increase earnings—that is, achieve more and strive for a better future, a better world. Recalling the introduction's discussion of incentives, the current income tax system imposes a negative incentive on performance and the higher paychecks there associated.

Though the countless lunacies of the current system could be lambasted *ad infinitum*, one final point to add is the manner in which taxes are collected. Limiting the discussion here to income tax, the approach is, in a word, complicated, but to add an appropriate qualifier, it is *absurdly* complicated and well beyond even the most liberal interpretations of sensibility, practicality, propriety, and humanity.

The first unjust burden falls to the employer—or heaven help you if you're self-employed—who is compelled to, under threat of severe punishment, withhold and report income to state and federal forces. Then, the employer must provide all of its employees with a statement that enables the next burden, the one that falls to the individual—filing taxes. The process is simple enough for an individual whose only income came as regular paychecks from a single employer. However, if other factors exist, the difficulties quickly compound into a Gordian knot of jargon-ridden forms and schedules. Spouses, children, tuition, interest, dividends, benefits, contract labor, short- and long-term capital gains, and a mountain of other common scenarios create an invidious nightmare for the humble taxpayer.

∼

Neuroscience is inherently complex, and so is quantum mechanics. By nature, some systems are intricate because of their sophisticated purposes. Taxes do not fall into this category. Mulcting the population and collecting taxes is not innately difficult, and yet it has become a vexatious and onerous effort for all parties involved. The fault lies with the helmsmen who are either fools or fiends, though most likely some combination thereof. They have created a system so gruelingly abstruse that few businesses or individuals can approach it on their own. Encouraged by threats of torturous audits and other legally sanctioned maltreatments, most choose to pay professional tax-filing services substantial remunerations. The current system is characterized not only by paying considerable taxes, but by *paying* to pay them.

Finally, the vast system that causes all these difficulties is extraordinarily expensive. In the same way that most of a rocket's fuel is used not to move the payload but the fuel itself, an unconscionable amount of effort, manpower, and—indeed—taxes are expended not for any purposeful cause, but for obtaining the tax itself. Surely, every taxpayer would feel better about his or her sacrifice if it at least went to some useful purpose and not to the process of taxation.

Prolepsis: Addressing commonly proposed alternatives

The previous sections dealt with the current system's faults, most of which can be rolled into complexity, brutality, and knavery. However, no diatribe is worthwhile unless it offers a practicable solution, and this chapter is no exception. Yet, before any such solution can be effectively treated, some commonly proposed alternatives must be analyzed, at least reductively. To address four of the most familiar:

1. **Raise/Lower taxes.** This is the most common proposal, the rote talking point of politicians across the board—top to bottom, left to right. While raising or lowering taxes might slightly intensify or allay the burdens felt by certain businesses or individuals, the proposal obviously does not address any of the fundamental flaws discussed above. This heartless grab at voters promises to solve nothing and, if implemented, have the same fleeting tenure as those who campaign on it.

2. **Tax by demographic.** This is the most divisive proposition, one that targets high earners, whether businesses or individuals, and is ill-conceived, unjust, and backed by political scheming and skulduggery. Directed at the rich, it claims that taxes should be paid by only those whose earnings exceed some threshold. The boundary is set around middle or upper-middle income—say, six-figures—with the pronouncement that people who earn so very much have more than enough to bankroll the rest of the population.

Aside from the immorality of this approach, its most contemptible features are its ignorance of human behavior, formal schism of the country into haves and have-nots, punishment for those who try to get ahead, incentivization of complacency, unrealistic accounting of expenses, and unfounded vilification of a segment of the population.

3. **Flat taxes.** This is the most levelheaded program. It would tax all people's income at a flat rate regardless of their earnings. For example, everyone owes 10 percent of their income, regardless of how many zeros are in one's salary. Fundamentally fair, this system eliminates the backward incentives of the current one. Nevertheless, it does little to address the copious variety of taxes and their many complications.

4. **Scandinavian-style socialism.** This is the most misunderstood proffer. It calls for the results of a system that it does not plan to adopt in fullness, nor realistically could. The Scandinavian countries are disparate from the United States in too many ways to count, not the least of which are their values and relatively homogeneous populations. Therefore, many of the foundations upon which their systems are built are impossible to reconstruct in the United States.

Even if the Scandinavian approach were attempted, there are several critical points that are often omitted from discussion. First, the highest-earning tax bracket is quite low, attainable by most of the population. The goal is not making only the rich contribute but requiring all self-supporting people to contribute an equal percentage. Second, all taxpayers receive the same governmental benefits, rich and poor alike. For example, the richest and poorest two people in the country both have access to fully-government-funded healthcare. Third, business is not unreasonably burdened. Since income and, consequently, taxes come through the wealth that the nation generates, businesses operate under a rather unencumbered tax system.

Unless these factors are considered and Americans unanimously agree to supplant their values with Scandinavian ones, that system will remain elusive. Half-hearted implementation will not lead to prosperity but to a privation-ridden destitution that is characteristic of every failed attempt at socialism.

The two-tax solution

This chapter's practical advice for a better world is a two-tax system. Envision a better world in which the great varieties of bewildering taxes are replaced by merely two—*demesne* (land) tax and *vendition* (purchase) tax. The concepts are straightforward. Demesne tax is a per-acre cost applied to land. Vendition tax is a percentage-based cost applied to purchased goods. Portions of both these will go toward all levels of government.

Though reminiscent of property and sales taxes under the current system, the proposed taxes should not be confused with them, as there are marked differences and, thus, go by different names. Concerning the proposed demesne land tax, the following contrasts to property tax are most noteworthy:

1. Demesne tax is uniform for an entire zip code. This allows for more-desirous areas to be taxed at higher rates but disallows the inane granularity associated with plot-by-plot property tax.

2. Demesne tax is informed only by zip code and acreage. Within the same vicinity, two same-sized plots of land

are charged the same. It does not matter if one is an unmaintained field and the other contains a fabulously groomed mansion.

3. Demesne tax cannot increase by more than 3.5 percent each year. Even in a municipality that increases its taxes annually and maximally, at the proposed 3.5-percent-per-year limit, one's property taxes will not double more frequently than once every twenty-one years.

The benefits of this proposal are several, but here are three:

1. Prevents sudden increases in property tax, which often makes one's land too expensive to retain.

2. Mitigates the nation's current plague of gentrification, meaning that long-time residents will not be forced from their land as wealthy newcomers skyrocket property values.

3. Eliminates punishment for improving one's property, because the land is taxed for its size, not the quality of the structures on it. Currently, a negative incentive exists that, if you make improvements to your house, you are taxed more because of it.

Vendition tax is similar to sales tax, but with necessary adjustments:

1. Tax-included prices. For consumer ease, the advertised price of goods and services should include all taxes. If the sign reads *ten dollars,* then a ten-dollar bill should be sufficient for the purchase. With the exception of gasoline, the current system is backward. A ten-dollar bill is rarely enough to purchase a product marked for

nine dollars and fifty cents. Consumers cannot make informed or wise decisions when factors such as final cost are withheld until the actual time of purchase.

2. A maximum limit. Whereas the nature of demesne tax made assigning an upper tax limit difficult, the percentage-based nature of vendition encourages such a condition. With respect to the untaxed purchase amount, all local taxes cannot exceed 10 percent, all state taxes cannot exceed 7 percent, and all federal taxes cannot exceed 7 percent. Even if the country, state, and municipality choose to tax at the highest permissible amounts, still only 24 percent—less than one-fourth—of the purchase amount can be charged as a tax. Therefore, a one-hundred-dollar item, pre-tax, will never cost more than one hundred twenty-four dollars post-tax.

Two points: First, the largest share goes to the local government, as it rightly should, because the local government fosters an environment that is or is not conducive to successful businesses and, therefore, should reap the largest reward. Also, the local government provides most of what people think about when they consider taxes: parks, schools, emergency services, roads, utilities, etc. These are wanted and needed by the population far more than many of the expenditures at higher levels of government.

Second, though a 24-percent purchase tax may feel costly indeed, consider that 24 percent is the *maximum* limit, not necessarily the one applied. Regardless, under the proposed two-tax system and the elimination of income and other taxes, one can expect to have a substantial increase in income, probably between 50 and 100 percent. (See "A Note on Feasibility" below for more.)

Like demesne tax, the proposed vendition tax has many benefits. Here are four:

1. Utilizes existing infrastructure. From multinational corporations to local cashier-and-calculator vendors, the framework for applying this simple tax is already in place. Only minor adjustments would need to be made to effectuate the new system.

2. Applies to everyone in the country. Whereas income tax is circumvented by under-the-counter labor and illicit money-making ranging vastly from babysitting to human trafficking, vendition tax applies to everyone who makes purchases, which is, more or less, every person, including students, retirees, illegal immigrants, vacationers from abroad, per-diem workers, extravagant millionaires, panhandling mendicants, and so on.

3. Applies fairly. Everyone pays an equal percentage regardless of their spending habits. Spendthrift top-one-percenters are charged at the same rate as frugal skinflints. Of course, though, as wealthy people make more purchases, they are indeed—in absolute dollars—paying far more toward taxes.

4. Allows for exceptions. For those who are concerned that vendition tax will increase the cost of necessities beyond what the poor can afford, the solution is simple—exempt the necessities. Though defining fundamental needs can lead to a slippery slope, reasonable concessions are warranted if they make the proposal more palatable. It is easy enough to exempt items such as medical care, medical supplies, groceries, utilities, vehicle maintenance, etc.

A note on feasibility

One of the likely questions to arise from this chapter is an exceedingly valid one: Can the proposed two-tax system cover the costs of government? This will be addressed momentarily, but a second question must be asked also: Does the current system? Since the United States has operated at a deficit for more than five decades, the second question's answer is boldly and unquestionably *No*.

Regarding this specific query, the proposed system has three benefits over the current one:

1. **It is cheaper to operate.** John Roebling's "100,000 spies," as quoted at this chapter's beginning, have no role in a two-tax system that can be managed by a fraction of the current operatives. No hours need to be wasted with bureaucratic scheming about the nuances of the current system or what minor changes should be made from year to year. There is no harassing the citizenry for tax forms and sorting through them; in fact, the reams of questionnaires, tables, forms, etc. do not need to be created at all. No elaborate systems of receiving and distributing money need to be established. No deductions exist to be audited. What used to be done by the myriad can now be done by the dozen. Right off the bat, annual expenses in the tens of billions of dollars—or probably much more—can be removed from the national balance sheet.

2. **It encourages growth of business.** The owner of a local convenient store spends far too much time on tax-related paperwork, and large businesses even more. Not only do corporations employ whole departments with the sole purpose of managing taxes, but the company's entire budget is usually informed by the same. Expenditure audits, especially those concerning capital and operational spending, restrict the business from operating in its best interest. Corporations cannot hire the amount of workers they desire nor grow their

services as inclined when doing so is accompanied by tax penalties.

Pure capitalism is fraught with malignancy, but Uncle Sam's scrutiny of every corporation and sorting each decision into high-tax and low-tax buckets is altogether worse. If businesses were liberated from their taxes, then they would be free to grow, hire, profit, and pass those profits to their employees. Note, also, that casting off corporate taxes is different from abolishing regulation altogether.

3. **It has potential to bolster government coffers.** The ineffable bliss of the two-tax system is nigh unimaginable. After income, sales, real estate, and personal property taxes have been paid, one's net holdings approach less than half of what the gross earnings were. Also, since those who have a little extra must save for their own medical expenses and retirement because the government's compulsory programs don't adequately serve them, the average person operates on a meager budget. For this tax-exhausted nation, there's little left to live on. In the mindset of each family's exiguous exchequer—half-empty wallet—the prospect of vendition tax becomes daunting, even if it were only one-half percent more than the current sales tax.

However, if the current system were not merely tweaked but wholly abolished and redesigned, then 100 percent of one's gross paycheck would go to the earner, and not a cent to taxes. At present, such an idea is practically inconceivable. Currently, people cannot multiply their hourly rate by forty and use that number when drafting their budget. However, the two-tax system is designed so that an employee salaried at fifty thousand dollars will have received fifty thousand dollars by year's end. And since rich and poor, legal and illegal, must buy necessities and *want* to make purchases that are presently unaffordable, national sales can be expected to soar.

From there, a positive feedback cycle can begin—people make purchases, businesses grow, businesses hire more employees, those employees buy what they want, and the cycle repeats. Additionally, since businesses would no longer be subjected to taxes of any form, other than demesne tax and forwarding vendition tax to the government, they are free to hire more employees, pay them more, increase their benefits, and reinvest back into the business to create better products.

Concerning feasibility, if the government feels budget-constrained, then it should first consider expanding tariffs on international goods. Instead of looking to increasingly tax its residents in every conceivable way—even after they die! (estate taxes, or death dues)—tariffs tax foreign merchandise entering the country. While curbing trade is far from ideal, tariffs, at least, do not actively stifle domestic businesses. In the runaway, worst-case scenario, foreign goods become too costly for everyday use and thus domestic industries have to expand to accommodate those needs. Contrast that outcome with the runaway, worst-case scenario of corporate taxes. Businesses can hardly maintain profitability and consequently outsource most production and labor to foreign countries, abandon United States soil altogether, or close. Neither outcome is salubrious, but a self-sustaining nation that produces its own goods is infinitely better than one in which few businesses—that is, few jobs—exist, and which has complete dependance on foreign powers. Sound familiar?

Vignette of a better world

Take a moment to imagine yourself as a product manager at a respectable thousand-employee company, and you are thankful to have the job. Two years earlier, the company indefinitely postponed four of the six projects that you were overseeing. The budget was there, and the company was eager to support your efforts because they felt that your department's projects would expand its market share and provide more value to its clients. Nevertheless, two-thirds of your projects were cut, along with an equal proportion of your department.

The layoffs were preemptive. The government had made a big to-do about increasing corporate taxes, and you had a front-row seat to that reality. Those at the chopping block were mostly young people getting their first work experience. Their projects were growth-focused, capitalized expenditures—retiring old software, streamlining systems, etc.—things that were unfavorably taxed. So, to play the corporate-tax game, the company doubled-down on its old model and bid part of its workforce farewell.

You remember struggling to find a job a few years earlier. No employer, it seemed, could afford to invest in anyone without extensive experience already. So, with your bachelor's degree, you lived a minimum-wage, hand-to-mouth existence. Finally, three years out of college, you managed to convince a company to give you a shot. You were ecstatic to be salaried well. Then, reality hit you when you received your first paycheck—over one-third went straight to taxes.

Nevertheless, you were still earning more than ever, and being an undaunted individual, you still budgeted for retirement, short-term investments, charitable donations, and saving for a home. Reality came hard once again when you filed for taxes. As it turned out, the government did not think that a cut of your paycheck was enough. Your bank interest and meager profits from the stock market were factored into your income, meaning that you owed more than you expected to. The icing on the cake was that you would have owed even more if you tried to deduct your charitable donations, since they were still well-below the standard deduction, so you ignored those and everything else you were told you could deduct and handed the IRS money that you were saving to fix your car's broken AC.

All in all, you felt a mixture of anger and foolishness, anger that your hard-earned money was taken from you without your consent—theft, by definition—and foolishness because you voted for the tax-loving politicians. You believed their specious arguments about making the rich pay more, but as an impecunious student you couldn't see the reality that it's not the rich who suffer, it's those who are trying to build a life for themselves. Apparently, your entry-level salary was considered *ultra-wealthy*.

But now, those days are past. Last year, the country adopted a two-tax system. Your company began investing in your department again. It could finally act on its designs for better products, and, as expected, the customers love it. You yourself are especially grateful because you can now spend more time focusing on your teams instead of spending a full day each week refactoring the budget to optimize corporate taxes. Better still, the company's number of employees exceeds what it was before layoffs, and it has made a policy of investing in junior talent.

Less than a week ago, you extended an offer to a promising young designer who won't even graduate college for another few weeks. The offer included a generous salary—what you were making not many years ago—but whereas that seemingly adequate salary was, after taxes, scarcely enough for you, it should be sufficient for your newest teammate to thrive.

As for you, you think about your own salary, which has increased substantially with your managerial role and the company's fresh success. You earn excellent income and see every cent of it deposited into your bank account. Knowing how much you spend and earn, you once again feel in control of your budget and, indeed, your life. If you were frugal enough, you could pay off your new house in just a couple of years. Before that, though, you want to plant a garden, build a deck, and repave the driveway. In a bygone era, you would never have considered upgrading your house since your property taxes would have jumped. But those days are past. The demesne tax cares about how much land you have, not what's on it, so you feel liberated to make your property better without fear of negative consequences.

Even though it's a new tax system, reality is still reality: your house projects are extensive, you love eating out, your car's AC conked again. After all these expenses and their associated vendition tax, you will still only have half your gross pay left over, but that happened on your own terms, not the government's.

Furthermore, feeling unbound by receiving your full salary, you allocate a fair amount to retirement and short-term investments. You are excited about both because all of their profits will go to you—not to taxes—though, of course, all of that money will find its way back to the economy through purchases and more investment. Finally, you can once again be generous with your money. You don't even need to try and limit yourself to what used to be known as a tax-deductible charity, a feature of the old tax system. You still give to those formal organizations, but you also feel better about other forms of generosity such as leaving bigger tips when you eat out, supporting a youth group's car wash, helping your nephew pay for college, and so many more acts of community kindness that the IRS—while that had existed—said didn't qualify as charity.

All things considered, you feel satisfied and empowered. You are satisfied with your contribution to taxes. Everyday purchases are slightly more expensive than they would have been under the old system, but you have twice the net income to spend. You have no problem with the idea of taxes—you never have. What used to bother you was the surfeit of them and the feeling of uncertainty that left you never knowing how much you would owe, what would be taxed, and if you were doing it correctly. But now you are satisfied with the process and relish its ease.

Most of all, you feel empowered to control your destiny. You can save if you want to save, spend if you want to spend. You can be generous with your money and not feel like you'll be punished for it come tax season. You can update your house and not be taxed more for the improvements. Your neighbors can improve theirs and not somehow burden you because of it. Most of all, you can plan for the future, and you plan to make it a good one.

CHAPTER 10

JUSTICE AND JURISPRUDENCE

> *We are not satisfied, and we will not be satisfied, until justice rolls down like waters, and righteousness like a mighty stream.*
>
> ~Martin Luther King, Jr.

> *The galleys make the convict what he is; reflect upon that, if you please. Before going to the galleys, I was a poor peasant, with very little intelligence, a sort of idiot; the galleys wrought a change in me. I was stupid; I became vicious: I was a block of wood; I became a firebrand. Later on, indulgence and kindness saved me, as severity had ruined me.*
>
> ~Victor Hugo, from *Les Misérables*

Philosophical questions

What is justice, and what system of jurisprudence can uphold it? Is law the great discriminant between order and chaos, between civilization and the wild? To what ends is it established, and by whose authority? Can laws be flexible? Can those who violate them ever be in the right? Is it possible for mankind to devise a system of true justice and recognize its arrival? Until such a time, how tightly shall we cling to an imperfect design?

Are laws designed to prevent wrong actions or to coerce right ones? Are punishments intended to force amends, to express disapproval, or to assuage damage? Is the purpose of a legal system to prosecute violations of laws, to defend rights, to arbitrate disputes, or to discover—through the process—what justice and jurisprudence truly are? Are prisons constructed to sequester criminals, punish them, or foster their eventual return to society? Do laws contain spirits, or are they but letters?

Systems of jurisprudence—whether at national or other levels—are some of the trickiest topics of investigation, for the discussion they invoke not only asks the questions above, but deeply probes the penetralia of our individual and collective beings, unearthing fundamental mores and philosophies about ethics, justice, virtue, mercy, and the most elemental notions of what it means to be a good person, a member of a society, and indeed what it means to be human.

Our legal systems and the laws that characterize them are the result of millennia's worth of scandent growth. Yet even before the first legal corpus or authoritative decree to the same, there has always been a fundamental sense of justice and morality. It is reasonable to wonder if those of good sense would even attempt to assess its foundations or anything other than its most superficial layer. The commentariat shifts uncomfortably when there is discussion about reevaluating individual laws. How much more will they writhe at the thought of reevaluating the system itself? And if we *do* start shifting stones, how easy will it be to differentiate between what is rotten and what is healthy? How will we identify what needs to stay and what needs to go? If we remove one brick because it is anachronistic or seems outdated, how likely is it that we will have destroyed a fundamental pillar of justice? Contrarily, are there pillars that masquerade as integral supports when they are nothing more than plaster facades?

While the average person might be ignorant of the innerworkings of an automobile, wholly unable to adequately describe even its basic components, almost anyone can recognize that grating screeching and noisy clanging are problems. Most people cannot diagnose and treat the way a physician does, but all people can recognize abject infirmity and declare *sickness* without the slightest uncertainty. In the same way, we can look at the current legal system and point out its flat tires and smoking engine and advise reasonable solutions without being intimidated by those who claim greater understanding than the average person.

Ignorance of the law

There is a maxim which avers, "Ignorance of the law is no excuse [for breaking the law]." In reality, ignorance of the law is both a reasonable and predictable excuse, or, better yet, explanation. Indeed, none—not even the most diligent student of the law—can be aware of even half their total number. When local, state, national, and worldwide governments employ panels and entire sessions of full-time lawmakers, how is anyone expected to be familiar with even an impressive fraction of them?

Of course, when it is used as more than simply a truncheon, the expression that "ignorance of the law is no excuse" can be thought of as a proverb, attempting to guide its audience into realizing that some violations are inherently—that is, intuitively—known. It does not take a legislator to tell someone that stealing is wrong, for base thievery is part of our moral fiber, our immanent legislation. For those who doubt that veracity, only let him or her suffer at the hands of theft to understand its outrageous wickedness. However, whatever verisimilitude this apothegm enjoys is quickly vitiated by the people who use it to convict those who transgress laws that are far beyond innate senses of right and wrong. It is akin to a mugger telling the victim that, "Life is not fair." Respond to that criminal, "Verily, life *can* be unfair, but in this case, it is *you*, not life, who precludes fairness."

Taking a broader scope, what do we do with a legal corpus so obese and overblown that it has become inscrutable and unknowable? Indeed, we have come far from Hammurabi's 282 edicts, or Moses's ten commandments. Granted, it is true that a vast swath of these laws will never be encountered by the average person, but the improbability of encountering a law does not assuage its prosecution.

But even more abundant are the laws that the average person *does* encounter daily. What consolation is given to the adolescents who ride their bikes to a lake and attempt fishing for the first time? Should they have known that they needed licenses to fish, that the one who forgot a helmet committed a misdemeanor? When new homeowners replace a broken outlet, how are they to know that the process requires permits and inspections? These supposed crimes are far from murder and theft. There are no instinctive aspects about them. When every part of life has a precept, every sliver a statute, where did the decrees diverge from sensibility?

First and foremost, if society's governing bodies are serious about the rule of law and enforce the belief that ignorance is no excuse, then they must also become serious about educating the population. Instead of burdening the individual and insisting that he or she, through personal effort and expense, somehow or other become knowledgeable about the vast world of law and all its subtleties, what if each household were furnished with a book of laws?

We know that any such effort would be an atrocious boondoggle, but consider it as a mental exercise. When volume one of fifty—all ten pounds of it—arrives at the door, what is that household to think? And suppose that the family were to actually sit at dinnertime and attempt to parse through that megillah's tedious argot and scholarly legalese? "Dear me," the reader would exclaim, "am I supposed to know all these, to abide by them? Half of these laws leave such room for extrapolation that, by these sorts of definitions, a dolphin is halfway to an elephant!"

When reading the collection, would the reader feel order or oppression? A soft and guiding hand, or a smothering and paternalistic one? Is the reader more likely to feel that lawmakers have been thorough, or that they have overstepped their proper scope?

Better still, deliver to the same doorstep a biannual list of updates—new laws that have been added, the revisions to preexisting ones, and—rarely, though possible—notifications that one or more have been removed. Let the family read that and be amazed by the astonishing frequency with which lawmakers create new legislation. Busy bees, these people are. Give them credit then and put their names next to the laws they voted to ratify, and then watch the outraged common folk remove them from the sacred offices they have violated.

Society has tried to fix its shortcomings through legislation. Laws and statutes can overcome discourteous neighbors, fix distracted drivers, remedy ineffective parenting, force awareness, surmount vice and debauchery, and effect the apotheosis of all who esteem it... or so the reasoning goes. But alas! These failings are not superable through legislation. The law has its proper utility, but it cannot replace virtue. For some inexplicable reason, though, those at society's helm have abandoned the latter and battened the former, hoping that with big enough, broad enough, extensive enough laws, we can somehow achieve utopia. Consider also that this explanation assumes that lawmakers are well-intentioned but misguided. How are we to contend with the more ignominious ilk who devise laws for personal power, profit, or worse?

Wishing that society were better is well and good, but we must also turn to practical advice. To address the unconscionable volume of laws, we can start with a twofold approach: First, begin by framing a proposed law in the context of criminality. Ask, "If someone were to break this law, should that person rightly be considered a lawbreaker—one who shuns decency and society, who deserves public disapprobation, who has wronged others? Is this person appropriately deemed *criminal*?"

Second, task lawmakers—some number between half and all of them—with abrogating current laws. Place addition on pause, and subtract from what currently exists. Approach the process using criminality as the first filter, then apply reasonable expectations as the second. Third, ask about the necessity of adding new laws, for if adding them were a weighty matter, and if the process were even half as difficult as defending oneself against alleged violations of those laws, then lawmakers would be forced to ask if they are really worth it. Does society *need* this thing implemented and enforced? Will it bring us closer to harmony? Or is it some preference, casually tossed, like so many others, onto an ever-growing heap?

Discipline and punishment

When someone has been convicted of a crime, the next question is what ought to be done with that person? A vast array of options is possible. Society can do nothing; or ask the criminal what he or she prefers; or offer something positive like a vacation; or something negative like jailtime, fines, or corporeal punishment; or, indeed, anything really. So first, we must ask, *What is our goal?* Indeed, we must ask why we even endure the process of prosecution and conviction. Is it merely to prove a hypothesis about who committed a crime, or is there an expectation that something happens if the hypothesis is proved?

Glossing over any pertinent philosophical argumentation, let us consider that there are two major goals: The first is to chasten, that is, to discipline with the goal of improving character or morals—in contrast to discipline for the sake of pure punishment. The second is to make amends, or put-to-right, if possible. Additionally, in the manifestation of these goals, let us assume the adage that the punishment be fitting the crime. Looking at the current system, there seem to be two prevailing punishments—*time* and *fine*. Time is, obviously, incarceration, and a fine is an amount of money that must be paid.

Concerning time: Avoiding discussion of any specific horrors imprisonment invites, its more-generalized problems are the following:

1. Although it punishes, it does not encourage improvement.

2. It offers no redress, either to individuals or to society, other than the circumstances in which society is best served by physically removing the criminal from it altogether.

3. It costs society dearly to confine the individual, especially if any decency is to be afforded to the criminal.

4. It effectively precludes his or her future reintegration into society.

For example, suppose an otherwise decent person—say, the manager at a grocery store—falls on tough times and chooses to embezzle money from the business. Eventually discovered and convicted, he is imprisoned three years. He has been removed from friends, family, and community for that duration of time, and surrounded by other criminals, some quite sordid. Upon release, is it more likely that his character and moral fiber will have strengthened or diminished? And, while he was sequestered, how did that confinement restore to the business that which was stolen? The store's owner and employees are glad that the theft has ceased and its perpetrator been penalized, but what amends are made? Furthermore, throughout those three years, although far from pampered, society has nevertheless paid for his food, lodging, clothing, medical care, entertainment, supervision, and much more. Perhaps more was invested in his punishment than was ever stolen by him. Lastly, upon return to society, what decent job can he hope to find? Will he obtain adequate housing or education or anything else? It is, after all, a society wherein most applications ask about one's criminal record. Can he ever put his misdeeds behind him, or is he fated for perpetual castigation as an ex-convict and scourge of society? Does anyone truly wonder why recidivism abounds?

Next, consider the punishment of fine. As with time, fines rarely chasten. There is a small chance that writing a check to the court will encourage contemplation or regret. Instead, it too is little more than punishment for the sake of punishment. It breeds resentment rather than reconciliation. Perhaps when the dust settles, funds will be available to the victims, but the truth is that many crimes cannot be atoned for with dollars, if anything. Another consideration of fines is that they punish the rich and the poor unequally. An amount that, for one person is trivial, is, for another, devastating.

So what better solutions are out there? Granted, not all punishments are appropriate for all crimes or criminals, but in general, punishments should be quick, impart a sense of poetic justice, offer a benefit to society, allow the offender to rejoin society after the punishment is complete, have equitable gravity across demographics and financial statuses, and attempt to make sufficient requital.

Consider the example of someone littering on the highway. That person is pulled over and fined some amount, say one hundred dollars. Though not a single person—rich or poor—wants to part with their hard-earned money, an affluent individual will likely not be set back by that amount, whereas someone who is just barely making ends meet will be crushed by it. In either case, that amount will cover neither the police officer's time nor any cleanup effort that may or may not even happen. In the end, the punishment might be negligible or might be severe, depending on the person's situation. In either case, there is little chance that the litter thrower will feel much remorse or consider repressing that behavior in the future. And, the requital to society *still* leaves society's budget in the red.

What if, instead of a fine, that person was sentenced to a cleanup detail. Imagine the offender joining a garbage-removal detail twice-a-week for a month. After several hours of picking up garbage along the highway, what is the result? First, time is far more equal across demographics than money—*equity*. It is true still, that in many cases, poor people will likely feel the weight more poignantly than their wealthy counterparts, but time will carry more gravity than money for either situation. Second, litter is removed—*requital*. Third, the offender is the one removing it—*poetic justice*. Fourth, it happens shortly after the crime, and then the encounter is over—*quick, and then rejoin society*.

In this example, it is the difference between sending a child to timeout to brood and build anger, verses making the child help clean up the mess and then accompany the parent to the store to purchase a replacement. In either case, the child may resent the parents and continue spilling milk, but the latter is constructive and yields better outcomes, so is it not the better option?

To offer another example, suppose the board of executives is convicted of knowingly polluting a city's water supply. Instead of simply paying a hefty fine, what if the punishment were more focused? First, by each convicted criminal sending—at their own expense—notices to affected residents explaining their action and its result. Perhaps they should also sponsor billboards and other public announcements to the same effect. Next, in addition to paying for whatever cleanup is required, the offenders must don their waterproof boots and accompany the cleanup crews to help with whatever testing or treatments are performed. They should be there at least once a week for the duration of the process.

Finally, let them not merely fix but *better* the water they sought to damage by planting flora that will improve water quality, sponsoring a nearby park or walkway, defraying maintenance costs at water treatment facilities, or anything else that leaves the place better than they found it.

In a situation like this, such criminals cannot get away with only a financial burden, which may or may not even cover the cost of repairs. And, with such a punishment, they cannot hide in anonymity and hope that few to none discover their ill deeds. Rather, if people's water has been tainted, they have a right to know which people, representing which company, did it. The offenders should be taught the scope of their crime, not by sententious bureaucrats, but by putting boots on the ground and joining the toil resultant from the crime. Finally, such a collection of criminals is prevented from writing a check and moving on while their victims endure a lengthy healing process. The offenders must take part in the struggle. However, once the process is complete, so is the punishment. Let it not linger forever.

Durance vile: The prison sentence

When considering punishments for lawbreaking, imprisonment deserves its own excursus. Herein, the discussion is substantially limited to only these two questions: What crimes are prison-worthy? What lengths of time are reasonable?

As mentioned previously, the current system of law heavily favors the utilization of time and fine as punishments. For cases wherewith *fine* alone seems an unworthy punishment, *time* is appended to the sentence. While avoiding creative penance is good practice and abides by the Eighth Amendment's guarantees—"excessive bail shall not be required, nor excessive fines imposed, nor cruel and unusual punishments inflicted"—this book invites penalties wherein the offender must fix, or help fix, that which has been damaged. Surely, it is not cruel to make the person who litters along the roadside help clear trash from the streets, nor is it cruel to make the person who pollutes drinking water go and witness how it is painstakingly corrected. This noted, when fine is not enough, perhaps there are indeed other possibilities than time.

In that case, who *should* get time, that is, what crimes are worthy of imprisonment? These are the ones in which the criminal has proved himself as a danger to society—murderers, kidnappers, abusers, violent thieves, and a bevy of others whose very presence places others at risk. For these people, sequestration and removal from society can be justified.

As to the duration of a sentence, this ought to be determined on a case-by-case basis, which it currently is. However, the unspoken reality is that the punishment lasts far longer than the imprisonment itself. First, there is the confinement itself. Second, there is parole, which is a sort of provisional allowance to rejoin society. If the parolee obeys the rules, freedom supposedly awaits, otherwise reimprisonment. Assuming that parole is well-tolerated, there is an unexpected third step: life as an ex-convict. This third stage is the one which lasts indefinitely.

Stage three is the barrier against creating a normal life. As previously alluded, housing, school, and the workforce frequently ask whether their applicants have been convicted of a felony. Many ask if the applicant has ever been *charged* with a felony, so much for the concept of innocent until proven guilty. Consequently, this mark of shame follows the ex-convict throughout life, precluding that individual from many of life's opportunities.

Recidivism is the phenomenon in which previously convicted criminals return to crime. It is rampant. Its prevailing causes are manifest and twofold—punishments that do not help address what turned the offender to crime, and inability to shed criminal status once it has been assigned. Now, some people proclaim that this stigma is righteous recompense for those who have committed crimes, that the crime's incessant lingering is part of a just punishment. Such thinking creates a permanent criminal class from which no escape is possible, and such a system certainly disserves society. It does not decrease crime, nor conserve resources, nor anything else useful to the non-criminals. Or, if all prison-worthy crimes are also life-sentence-worthy, then make it so, and forego the humiliating taunt of parole, hope, and eventual recidivism.

What is the goal of punishment, particularly imprisonment? Is there an expectation—or even a possibility—of returning to society? Can one's crimes ever be left in the past?

If the answer is no—that one's crimes must follow that person to the grave or beyond—then the current system is in fine fettle and has been adequately calibrated. On the other hand, if we, as a society, believe that the matter should be concluded once a person has fulfilled his appointed punishment, then the current system is malfunctioning.

Given the latter philosophy, the criminal-justice system needs to be redesigned to fashion punishments that sufficiently fulfill their intended purposes, and then are concluded. If the punishment is fine or time, or something else, then sobeit. If a period of reintegration—such as parole—is deemed necessary, then incorporate that. Once all obligations are met, then let that person be reinstated as a full-fledged member of society.

The for-profit legal system

If a fire department were paid by the minute when extinguishing fires, we would expect certain firefighters to go about town starting blazes, responding to them, and taking their sweet time to douse the flames. Such a paid-by-the-minute system would incentivize that behavior and design a world in which—from the firefighters' financial perspective—fires are good, and their absence is bad. Thankfully, we do not utilize that backward system. As is, firefighters try to prevent fires, and when they do occur, these exemplary people work hard to quench the infernos as quickly and safely as possible. The first scenario described a type of for-profit system. In many industries, the allure of profit encourages people to work harder, push the limits of their creativity, and strive toward that reward. However, in other areas, it can invite ignominious practices.

Lawyers must work hard to master the law and help others navigate it, and they deserve worthy compensation for that effort. Nevertheless, the current for-profit nature of the legal system is surely one of its greatest shortcomings. Is there a balance between year-upon-year of laborious study and a role which, in many respects, is one of public service? Whoever finds the solutions first—lawyers or physicians—should inform the other without delay.

Regardless, given the current system, certain types of lawyers are incentivized to create problems, argue on behalf of ridiculous claims, and avoid assessing right and wrong. Think about the legal sleight of hand that allows companies to obtain and sell others' data. Think about the chicanery that allows contracts to overwhelm those who are told to sign them. If winning cases and working for corporate giants were not so lucrative, would lawyers still support their unjust demands? If a trial lawyer received the same amount whether clients won or lost, would so many absurd cases be supported?

∽

The purpose of law, and the manifestations it should assume, invite enthralling philosophical debates. Setting aside these discussions, let us posit that the fundamental reason for law is to set forth, extend, and grant consistency to every human's innate sense of right and wrong, of justice and injustice. Under this reasoning, the law does not exist for itself. It is not a supreme being, but a servant. It is not, therefore, a riddle nor a puzzle nor a game that encourages its players to exploit loopholes and uncertainties. It is not an abstract work of art, inviting any and all interpretations. It is not a cudgel designed to intimidate or oppress, nor a challenge seeking to be overcome by the strong and clever.

Jurisprudence, like many of the monoliths on which our society depends, is rarely reassessed, but all arrangements need maintenance and updates. Engaging with the system should feel like riding a sleek, agile train to a known destination, the riders' fees having been nominal. Instead, it is a clunky, smoke-billowing engine from a previous era, slowly and nauseatingly carrying its riders to unknow, unintended, and undesirous destinations for one hefty fee and many smaller costs along the way.

First, we need to return to fundamentals and define the purpose and scope of law. We need to reduce the legal corpus to a manageable size, notably by asking what really ought to be enshrined as rules for society. If laws were carved in stone, what would be worth the stonecutter's effort? For the ideals we choose to instantiate as laws, what punishments are sensible for those who transgress them? And, of the punishments that are finite, how can we ensure that once penance is made, absolution is given? Finally, how can we dismiss any for-profit aspects of the system, along with the associated scheming and ignominy it invites?

Happy are we, then, that these decisions do not belong to a monarch or council or class or any of the other entities in which the power of law has historically been vested. We can, and must, elevate leaders and lawmakers who value righteousness and justice—good people who are committed to raising purposeful institutions guided by the same. In the words of the prophet Amos, "Let justice roll down like waters, and righteousness like an ever-flowing stream." (Amos 5:24, ESV)

CHAPTER 11

AID AND ADMINICLE

> *If at age 20 you are not a Communist then you have no heart. If at age 30 you are not a Capitalist then you have no brains.*
>
> ~George Bernard Shaw

> *The problem with socialism is that you eventually run out of other people's money.*
>
> ~Margaret Thatcher

Introduction and philosophical concerns

If it is true that a society is judged by its treatment of its needy, and if it is also true that we value compassion, charity, and other such virtues, then it naturally follows that we, as a people, must strive to help those among us who cannot help themselves. With this in mind, we have our guidance. However, the hell of reality is its complexity, and the concerns of aid and adminicle deserve a more appropriate discussion than the one just provided.

It is easy to isolate the cause of charity and elevate it as an irreproachable touchstone, but the same can be said about how we—collectively—treat children, animals, the unpopular, the environment, or any number of other groups or things, including justice. And, when considering justice, we must contend with the ramifications of taking from those who have and giving to those who don't.

This, after all, is the notion behind government aid. It is not charity. Charitable efforts are decisions made by individuals who have the capacity to decide which charities they support and when to increase or decrease that furtherance. Charity occurs when self-determinant people voluntarily choose to set aside a portion of what they have and give it away. Contrast this to government aid, wherein those from whom the resources arise have little or no voluntary choice, ability to withhold, determination about allocations and distributions, or really any qualities of pure charity. Other than half-hearted arguments about *voicing with one's vote*, government aid is most-appropriately viewed as taking rather than giving. Notwithstanding, this should not preclude consideration of appropriate opportunities for governing bodies to allocate portions of their budgets to aid. First, though, we must address the pertinent concerns. Government aid is not necessarily inappropriate, but it is not the fundamental reason for government. If it were, then the government's overriding objective would be ridding its territories of poverty and all other wants. Noble and desirous though this is, it is accompanied by at least two very serious hesitations: Does it have potential to incentivize neediness and disincentivize self-support? Is compulsory *giving* ethical?

To the first hesitation: In an extreme scenario, in which a government fulfilled all wants, the natural necessity to get oneself up and going—to provide for oneself—is removed. In the absence of that external motivation, only internal motivation compels a person to move beyond what the government provides. If the government enforced some sort of external, perhaps punitive, motivation, then many would incur that measure and be denied the aid, thereby contradicting the idea that the government alleviates all wants. In such a case, it is no different than holding a job in a world without charity. For those motivated to rise above the level of government aid, their efforts would yield diminishing returns as their marginal gains become distributed across the masses.

To the second hesitation: Is it just to take from Person A and give to Person B? To aver that such an arrangement is just or fair naturally assumes that Person A has whatever resources at the expense of Person B. For example, Person A accumulating wealth through the mistreatment of Person B. In that circumstance, taking from A and giving to B restores balance and order, albeit delayed and through unideal means. In some, perhaps many, cases, this is true, and just maybe all such Persons A owe far more to their Persons B than necessities only. However, we cannot reasonably argue that all people with means acquired those means at the expense of others. Furthermore, this assumes that *Person B* was victimized by *Person A*. What if, instead, Person A earned a living on the back of a Person C? If we then take from A and give to B, where is the justice for C, and is it not true that B is just as guilty now, if not possibly more, than A?

In short, compulsory giving cannot be deemed just. Implementation of such systems must be carefully weighed against the government's duty to protect its citizen rights. However, here it is important to distinguish between natural (negative/do not) rights and accorded (positive/do) rights.

Natural rights prevent infringement whereas accorded rights ensure help. For example, consider the right to property. The natural right means that the government cannot prevent you from purchasing land and owning it. The accorded right says that you must have land, and that anything in the way violates that right. In the first case, you must either find someone willing to gift you property, or you must pay for it yourself. You are not entitled to land. In the second case, the land is your inherent right, whether or not you can find a seller. Therefore, anyone refusing to sell or give you land violates that right. Another example: A natural right to free speech means that you cannot be stifled from speaking your opinion. An accorded right means that others are forced to listen.

In this light, if we assert that people have an inherent right to be free from abject wants, then there are two interpretations: First, the natural right prohibiting the government from disallowing a person meet his or her necessities. Second, the accorded right allowing a person to take from others to meet his or her necessities. Worthy, humane, and respectable governments protect only the first, as well as all natural rights.

The needy

When an individual supports a charity, he or she freely chooses who to help, for what reasons, in what manner, and over what duration. Since government aid depends on *taking*, it must exist within strict parameters that are unambiguously defensible. The circumstances warranting aid cannot be excessive. Rather, they must be dreadful enough that the act of *not giving* viscerally shames society and tarnishes the species.

First and foremost, aid should be limited to circumstances in which the ability to continue on with life is untenable. Another way to frame this idea is that aid should address needs rather than wants. Accordingly, aid must be given to those whose needs are currently unmet. Of such individuals, there are two broad categories—those who *cannot* provide their own needs, and those who *choose not to*.

Since interpreting another's ability versus willpower is not only a matter of external opinion, but also subject to poorly understood factors, especially mental ability and other topics better left to psychologists and similar doyens of that domain, the lines between those who *cannot* and those who *will not* are blurry and given to constant evolution. Since the practicalities of differentiating the two groups are imperfect at best, in this light, we can only acknowledge that aid *should* be reserved for those who *cannot* support themselves, and that it should be denied to those who can but choose not to. Therefore, for the sake of definition, let *the needy* be those determined to have unmet necessities owing to their *inability* to self-support.

Concerning the needy, we must also ask if such support should have a maximum duration or, separately, causes for disqualification. While the vastness of each unique possibility is beyond comprehension, a reasonable place to begin is acknowledging that when a person no longer meets the criteria for aid, he or she should no longer receive it. For example, suppose a critically ill person was unable to support herself due to that illness, so at that time she qualified for aid. When she has recovered and returns to work or otherwise can meet her own necessities once again, she should stop receiving aid.

Charity: The ideal state

The pages of this book are dedicated to the pursuit of a better world. Not the best, mind you, but one that sets us on the path. However, it is worth taking a momentary aside to ask about that best world, or one much nearer to it. Indeed, in relation to this chapter's content, the best world would be free from abject wants, unmet necessities, and all evils that cause privation. Perhaps future technology and other means will make that dream a reality, and at that time this chapter will, happily, fade into irrelevance.

Until that elysian age, the next-best world is one in which charities supplant the need for government aid. Ideally, people with means would be sufficiently willing and generous toward those without. There would be nothing for the government to provide since all needs would have already been met by others. For this to happen, several factors need to align:

1. The ability to meet and exceed one's own needs must be unencumbered, to the point that working-class people feel that they have excess to give.

2. The government must not stifle the first factor. For this objective, there must be a healthy environment for businesses to thrive, employ, bolster, and produce. Accordingly, excessive regulation and taxation on both businesses and individuals must decrease.

3. The needy must truly fit that definition. Most people are naturally kindhearted and wish to help those who need helping hands; however, most self-supporters also abhor those who can support themselves but refuse to. To create a society that is eager to give, those requesting charity must sincerely need it. *Lazy beggars*, as it were, should be discouraged lest those with the ability to lend support become jaded, desensitized, and unwilling to help.

4. By far the most important: Those who tout charity—particularly religious organizations—must live up to their proclamations. Several religions extol charitable giving as a fundamental virtue, perhaps none more than Christianity. In this idealistic vision of the world, churches of all ilk and their members would compete in these good works. No longer would charity be small slivers of the budgets, but the very largest pieces, to the point that the government would have no void to fill because private entities will have already met and exceeded whatever needs were there.

All in all, the best versions of the world would have no government aid whatsoever because another entity would have earlier accomplished what government aid was intended to do.

Possible entities can take many forms, most notably science and technology, individuals with means, charitable organizations, and religious institutions.

Aid: The current state

Prevenient to envisioning a better world's version of aid, we must identify some broad characteristics of the current system. Government aid is vast, varied, and difficult to evaluate. Misleading names and categories exacerbate this frustration; for example, in the United States, programs like Social Security, unemployment, Medicare, and Medicaid are generally grouped together as *benefits* or *entitlements*. However, consider that Social Security is a compulsory, federally run retirement plan and not a handout, since people are forced to pay into it even though most, if it were voluntary, would probably choose another option. Unemployment is primarily funded by employers obliged to make compulsory payments to the government for this purpose. It is difficult to categorize this as a handout because it is, in essence, a mandatory insurance program paid by working people before their salaries can even be calculated. Medicare is federally managed health insurance that members pay for, though is heavily subsidized by the government. It is a gray area, particularly given its massive stranglehold on the healthcare system and power to control the same, including its ability determine healthcare costs for the entire system, making the need for *government medical insurance* a self-fulfilling prophesy. Finally, Medicaid is, in essence, government coverage of medical costs; as such, it is a true handout, not funded by those who receive it.

These examples illustrate one of the hallmarks of the current system; that is a vast proportion of government *aid* is comprised by quasi-obligatory, partially subsidized programs that have, or would have, a preferable free-market counterpart. For example, there is the government-mandated retirement plan called Social Security, and there are private methods of planning and saving for retirement. The former takes from people who have more and gives to those with less, creating a somewhat homogenous distribution that is insufficient for everyone, whereas the latter is designed by those who use it to fully meet future expenses.

If only Social Security existed, there would be insufficient funds for all. However, if only private/personal retirement strategies existed, then those who have such strategies in place would meet their own needs, and those who do not could be considered for a pure form of aid.

When comparing these two possibilities, which we can refer to as *governmental* and *private* means, they look like different ways to still not accomplish the end goal, which, in this example, is creating a system in which no one starves in their twilight years. A governmental programs takes paint from everybody's garages, stirs it together, and covers as many houses as possible with a thin coat the same color. Private programs allow those with their own paint to coat their houses with as much of whatever color they choose, but then does not necessarily address those without their own paint who cannot color their houses. So, which is worse? Everyone with unfinished jobs, or some with completed efforts and some with little or nothing to show altogether?

Governmental is worse, and here are some of the reasons why:

1. A sizable portion of the total expenses are operational and do not contribute to the end goal. There is extensive bureaucratic sludge that consumes many of the total resources.

2. Everyone succeeds, or, in almost all cases, fails together, allowing no diversity of outcome.

3. There is no consideration of personal situation or

preference, nor acknowledgment that different people have different needs.

4. There is no freedom of choice to opt in or out, or to what degree.

5. The arrangement of *taking and redistributing* rather than *giving and receiving* fosters contempt from each side toward the other.

6. The people who fund the system, that is, the people with means, who receive less than they contribute, are continually disincentivized to acquire their extra means because their end result will be the same as everyone else's.

7. The people who fund the system retain little desire to lend additional support to others because they have already been forced to help once.

8. The people *who do not* fund the system, that is, the people without means, who receive more than they contribute, feel cheated when the people *who do* fund the system have anything left over with which to set themselves apart and give the impression of wealth.

The items enumerated above highlight many of the current system's shortcomings, though, of course, the list is severely incomplete. Nevertheless, in such a vast arena, seemingly all possible outcomes are represented; inasmuch, it is unfair to assert that the current system of government aid accomplishes no good works. Indeed, people are fed, housed, educated, and taken care of in many ways, so the system is not incontrovertibly useless.

However, we must not lose sight of the means by which the

ends are accomplished, and what those ends even are. Currently, the means are those listed above, broadly characterized by gross inefficiency, compulsion, inadequacy, divisiveness. The ends are natural outcomes of the means, including pyrrhic partial victories, generalized deficits but not dire privation, low-level hostility between different demographics, and a bevy of self-fulfilling declarations including these: The current amount of aid is inadequate for the task at hand, the available resources are too few, needy people are spineless good-for-nothings, wealthy people are heartless good-for-nothings, and government managers are brainless good-for-nothings.

The final note about the current state is its disheartening ability to force dependency and deter upward mobility. Whether through happenstance or malicious design, people who receive true aid do not easily emerge from that mendicant status into the more fulfilling ones of self-supporters, contributors, etc. The direct cause of this phenomenon is the hard cutoffs which differentiate those who are eligible for aid and those who are not.

Consider this fictitious illustration of a two-adult, two-child household in which neither adult earns an income. Having no income, the family is given government housing, food stamps, school breakfasts/lunches, Medicaid, transportation stipends, and more. Tired of living this way and wanting better lives and the ability to give rather than take, the adults pursue scholarships, attend trade school, get jobs, and work hard to rise above the need for aid. Together, they gross $40,000 for the year and have a bright future on the horizon.

But lo! The aid bracket was a combined income of $30,000, so now the family is ineligible for aid. They now pay taxes—federal, state, Social Security, Medicare, sales, property, etc.—on their income, amounting to 25 percent of their pay. Their spare money is down to $30,000. Housing costs half of the remainder; down to $15,000. Food costs one-third; down to $5,000.

Transportation—a used car, fuel, insurance, and maintenance for one; bus passes for the other—amount to one-tenth; down to $2,000. Medical insurance and medical expenses are one-twentieth; down to $500. The other desires of life quickly consume the remainder.

In the end, the family looked at its situation and determined the following: Whether in these roles or unemployed and receiving aid, their necessities were met, but the quality was bottom of the barrel. Either way, there was little to nothing left over. On aid, they had free time during the day and little administrative overhead to manage their lives. With jobs, the lion's share of their waking hours was spent commuting to, and being at, entry-level jobs that left much to be desired, and the administrative overhead of their lives was significant. Furthermore, the ability to afford nicer housing, vehicles, clothes, etc. would likely require about double their income, but at that point they would be taxed even more and be eligible for even fewer benefits, not the least of which is the prospect of higher education, should their children pursue those routes. At that point, it might take two jobs for each adult to cover the expenses that unemployment and aid would manage. In the end, aid seems like the better deal, and they are not wrong.

This reductive example is a caricature of a very real occurrence. In many cases, receiving aid is a better prospect than supporting oneself, because the cusp of transition results in a significant shock that yields few returns. In short, getting off of aid—upward mobility, as it were—is discouraged.

Adminicle: The better state

The systems of aid in a better world would function differently enough from their contemporary counterparts that they deserve a distinct name—*adminicle*. Adminicle is essentially synonymous with aid/help/support, etc. and, in this context, is a proposed outline for an altogether enhanced system of government aid.

For added clarification, let us refer to those who fund adminicle or receive less than they provide as *begetters*; similarly, let us refer to those who receive as *cadgers*, since "to cadge" is to take, receive, or beg without intent to repay.

Adminicle can be differentiated from contemporary aid in the following ways:

1. **Adminicle is grave.** To rationalize the unfair, perhaps even unjust, arrangement in which begetters are forced to yield their resources to cadgers, we must ensure that whatever is given as adminicle obviates dire situations. These must be situations of true need—hunger, thirst, exposure, and other abject horrors, the presence of which would undermine whatever other triumphs our society attains. Adminicle is a final safeguard against privation, to maintain support even when charity and goodwill may fail.

   Of course, the direness of adminicle does not mean that loftier charities should not exist, nor, for that matter, charities that address the most basic needs. If certain people desire to fund an organization that gives people who own five pairs of shoes a sixth pair, then they are free to do so with conviction. But should the government be in the business of providing excess to those who already have the minimum? It cannot be, lest it defeats its own reason for existence—the protection of rights. Adminicle makes allowance for those rights to be bent or, frankly, ignored—to take from begetters whether they want to give or not. We can justify this to keep other human beings in a livable state, but we cannot justify it to simply give things away. Provide food? Yes, that is reasonable. Provide delicacies? That is the business of charity. Provide safe shelter? Yes, so dictates human decency. Furnish it with fine decorations and entertaining gadgets? That is beyond governmental purview.

2. **Adminicle is precative.** When a person is lacking life's basic requirements, he or she must only ask for help to receive it. The key is to ask. The purpose of this precatory restriction is to attempt to limit adminicle to only those who actually need it, who notice something missing from their livelihoods. This is not an exercise in shame, deference, or any such ignoble humiliation. But it should never be the case that a person receives a check in the mail and discovers that he or she, unbeknownst until now, qualifies for a certain type of aid and is now receiving it.

    Adminicle is not the practice of handing out *free* money—begetters' money, that is. As such, it should never blanketly apply to an entire neighborhood, occupation, race, generation, or any other demographic passel. Neither should the government attempt to seek out people who might qualify for adminicle and offer that handout in expectation of a recipient's need. Although few people would turn away money or any other manifestation of adminicle, how many of those targeted individuals would have been in such dire need of it that they would have gone to some government facility to ask for it?

3. **Adminicle is consolidated.** People who qualify for adminicle shouldn't have to endure the hassle of separately navigating, qualifying, applying for, etc. each facet that is available. And, because of the nature of adminicle and the purpose it serves, an overabundance of subsets simply does not exist. Instead of a multiplicity of government agencies vomiting a flurry of programs with excesses of nuanced candidates, criteria, applications, and disbursements, there should be a single entity, say, the

Secretariat of Adminicle, which manages a streamlined, accessible process governing all its concerns.

One possible manifestation of this principle it that, upon qualifying for adminicle, a person receives coupon-like items called *adminicle defrayments*. These compose the entire assistance rendered and are similar to checks written on the government's treasury, so that they are easily *cashed* by the retailers who receive them. There is one for an amount of groceries, one covering a portion of each critical utility bill up to a maximum amount, one for an amount of clothing, one for a portion of rent or mortgage up to a maximum amount, one for public transportation, and perhaps a small number of other necessities warranted by the state of society's many industries, most notably healthcare.

4. **Adminicle is salutary.** Whether rearing children, caring for the poor, or mentoring professionals, there is always the caution to ask when helping starts to hurt. Though each situation is different, the general goal of keeping help helpful always applies. As such, adminicle should prioritize being salutary—beneficial or helpful. And, though a neutral outcome points to many wasted resources, adminicle should never be allowed to become desultory or harmful the way that current aid has become. In short, adminicle should accomplish a positive end, but at the very least, do not let it make things worse or hurt the cadger who receives it. Especially, adminicle needs to be designed so that people can, and are encouraged to, overcome their dependance on it and strive toward self-support, begetting, voluntary charity, and beyond.

The easiest way to ensure this is to make adminicle expire or rapidly decrease after very few months, potentially just one or two, and non-renewable for a given period of time. This would be similar to how unemployment works, though in a way that does not encourage blatant abuse. Of course, there are potential undesirable repercussions of letting adminicle expire, particularly those who have permanent disabilities that preclude self-support, but such special circumstances can be accounted for, most obviously by allowing them to waive adminicle's expiration. Also, in the spirit of helping people wean off of adminicle and emerge into success, rendered support should decrease over time rather than stop suddenly.

5. **Adminicle is subaltern.** This is to say that receiving adminicle should never be better than not receiving it. No person should look at their self-support, then at adminicle, and determine that adminicle would be preferable. If that happens, adminicle and the government that promulgates it have failed the citizenry and incentivized an entire society to forsake yearning, dreaming, and personal industry in favor of becoming beggars and dependents.

This does not mean that adminicle should furnish its recipients with loathsome ersatz of real support—torn clothing, moldy bread, damp and dilapidated lodging. Rather, it means that adminicle should provide only just enough, and not more: dignified, clean clothing, yes, but not designer labels; food that is edible, nutritious, and even tasty, yes, but not fine dining; housing that is safe and sturdy, yes, but not necessarily stylish, and not any safer or sturdier than a working-class person can hope to attain. Remember that adminicle exists to overcome needs. For begetters who wish that cadgers were given more than the minimum, those magnanimous people are at liberty, and encouraged, to make it happen through private means. It is perfectly acceptable for a group to arise and create a charity which offers the finer things in life, to the point that receiving that charity exceeds what most people can achieve through gainful employment. But as far as adminicle is concerned, receiving it is never better than not needing it in the first place.

Final considerations

A perfect world would have no unanswered wants, but this hopeful bubble is popped by the real world wherein there are complex networks of cause-and-effect poised to upset naïve idealism. Shaw's quote at the beginning of this chapter is stunningly spot-on: "If at age 20 you are not a Communist then you have no heart. If at age 30 you are not a Capitalist then you have no brains."

Young adults on the cusp of creating their own lives believe that if everyone were a bit kinder and willing to share just a little, then there would have no wants; hence everyone would be provided for. This sanguine vision of the world is refreshing and laudable, but after ten or twenty years of hard work, trying to build up one's personal concerns and family, and attaining a broader vantage of the world, the deceptive sophistry of communism begins to crack and give way to harsher-sounding capitalism.

Not that either of these systems is without fault, but incentives are real motivators that do exist and are not easily overcome. For aid and adminicle, their most dangerous unintended consequences relate to their ability to incentivize and disincentivize. These aspects of human nature are not identified to cast people in a bad light, but merely to assert facts.

When there are two roads, we choose the easier option. If one can arrive at the same end through working many hours a week or none whatsoever, sensible people choose the option of not working. Even zealous achievers would choose not to work, not owing laziness, but because then they could put that time toward other projects. As such, incentivization is not a shortcoming of our species, but simply a reality, and since it exists, we can ask about aid's more pronounced concerns, several of which have been alluded to previously. Namely:

1. Sometimes what is intended to help actually hurts those who receive it. Generally, pure handouts are ill-advised. Structured support, which involves helpers taking active roles in the lives of the helped, yields better results.

2. Excessive taxation for the intention of creating more *charity* creates a feedback loop, which overall reduces charity. To offer more of an explanation: If the government assumes that people are misers who will not willingly help others in need and, riding that train of thought, taxes its citizenry for the purpose of then giving it away as aid, then people will have less to give and feel less compelled to give it, thus decreasing the overall private contributions toward charitable ends. Seeing this, the government might tax even more. Then even less will be given outside of what is taxed. The government will subsequently offer this as proof of its original assumption that people do not give of their own volition. In contrast, however, the average person is actually happy to sacrifice a portion of their resources to help others. After excessive taxation, though, which leaves many people's net incomes overstretched, few people feel that they have enough to give, and some of those who can choose not to because they have already contributed through taxation.

In short, we cannot look to the charity offered by a taxed population to make determinations about what their charitable contributions would be if untaxed.

3. If aid were persistent, or if it were too good, then there would be no incentive to leave it. One could argue that aid should be indefinite and high-quality while a person needs it, but if you knew that the government would buy your food-of-preference and cover your necessary expenses for the rest of your life, then why bother with the hard work of affording those things yourself? This does not make you lazy, but sensible. To avoid unintentionally offering this *disincentive*, aid should decrease prior to finally expiring at a certain reasonable point, and not be a better prospect than self-support.

   Unemployment is a startling example of how aid can be abused. When unemployment during 2020 and the ensuing years was battened, increased to an amount greater than the average working person's wages, and offered for an indefinite period of time, even people with decent jobs quit them in favor of unemployment. It was more money for no work, particularly during a time when working conditions were more stressful than usual. Under such circumstances, few people can find reasons to stay at their jobs. *Unintended consequences* like these are predictable and, in a properly structured system, avoidable.

There are three additional considerations that are worth note:

1. Should aid that is given be given to all? For example, suppose that the current system of aid gives people within a certain low-income threshold a monthly food stipend. Because everyone spends money on food, there is an

inherent incentive for all people to abandon their means of self-support and attempt to qualify for the stipend. To avoid that situation, there are at least two options. The first is to limit that stipend in both amount and duration, preventing it from becoming a permanent means of support. The second is to offer everyone that incentive; that is, give the same stipend to everyone and anyone. However, when the floor is raised in such a manner, so too is everything else in the room. It is akin to rapid inflation. The stipend would quickly become worthless as the value of money decreases. Then, we are back to the same starting point, but after having expended much to get there.

2. Should aid be given to non-citizens? This question is best left to the citizenry that would be implementing aid or adminicle in their lands, but it is worth serious consideration. On the one hand, we don't want to see unfed people, whether they are citizens or not. A human in need is a human in need. But on the other hand, government aid programs are profoundly more extensive than offering a single meal to a one-time starving beggar. They require substantial resources and infrastructure. Ideally, we would like to help everyone in need, but we must first ask about our own household. It is not right for parents to let their own children starve because they are busy feeding other families. A nation must ask about its own people prior to asking about others. (For a more thorough discussion about citizens, non-citizens, when the latter should become the former, the differences between the two, and why the current system is grossly inadequate, consult the chapter "Pathways to Citizenship.")

3. Should any of this matter? Yes, because resources are finite, because people must work hard to create what the world consumes, and because everyone needs a helping hand now and again. However, if concerns like production and resources were no longer relevant due to advanced technology, or if private charity were allowed to thrive and unseat government aid, then the content of this chapter would, with joy and gladness, become irrelevant. To put it bluntly, all of this would be thrown out the window.

CHAPTER 12

STATES OF EMERGENCY

> *Immediate necessity makes many things convenient, which if continued would grow into oppressions.*
>
> ~Thomas Paine, from *Common Sense*

> *When martial law rages, insanity becomes the norm.*
>
> ~James Michener, from *Caribbean*

Overview and introduction

States of emergency are always serious affairs. They are accompanied by fear, damage, and loss of liberty; therefore, they must be considered with reservation, initiated with intention, implemented with prudence, prolonged with scruple, and terminated with celerity.

The specific form assumed by each state of emergency is different because of cause (weather, disease, terrorism, etc.), level of implementation (local, state, national), and a bevy of other factors such as leadership, locality, and resources. Nevertheless, all effective states of emergency have the following attributes:

1. **Rarity.** The adage, "When everything is urgent, nothing is urgent," is apodictic; therefore, declarations of emergency must be infrequent enough to lend their

existences credibility. If they are frequent or regular, then they are not—or, in some cases, cannot be—regarded seriously or executed productively. Furthermore, if regularity is the motif, it begs the question of what constitutes a true emergency? And if a true emergency appears lacking, are states of emergency merely excuses for despotic limitations of rights?

2. **Clarity.** States of emergency must have clear reasons for existence, precise policies, and defined criteria for termination. It is unacceptable for people to not know why an emergency has been declared, what changes are happening during the emergency, or what determines when that emergency has passed.

3. **Legerity.** Leaders must be capable of acting on their feet and handling evolving situations. Rigid processes will quickly become irrelevant and, potentially, counterproductive if adhered to blindly or thoughtlessly. The rationale must always aim toward resolving a distinct real and present emergency, not treating a hypothetical one.

4. **Rapidity.** Emergencies are, definitionally, quick. An emergency cannot last for extended periods of time even if its effects are persistent.

5. **Territory.** States of emergency must be applied to only those affected by the emergency. For example, severe weather affecting one part of a state might not affect other parts. Declaring that the entire state will be under a state of emergency is unjustifiable.

The terminology used in this chapter is generic, so to enhance clarification, note that:

- The *executive* refers to the head of the executive branch of government—mayor at the local level, governor at state, president at national.

- The *legislature* refers to the legislative body at a given level of government—city council at local, legislature at state, Congress at national.

- *Coequal* refers to an executive and legislature that are of the same level of government.

- From *low/lower* to *high/higher*, the levels of government are local, state, national.

Phases of emergencies

State of emergency can be usefully divided into five phases, each of which deserves individual treatment. They are *consideration, initiation, implementation, prolongation,* and *termination.*

Consideration is the planning phase. Each level of government has a duty to its citizens to regularly evaluate, rehearse, and otherwise prepare for diverse emergencies. Weather (floods, hurricanes, fires, landslides), infrastructure failure (bridge collapses, dam failures, sinkholes), scarcities (shortages of food, fuel, medicine), mass-casualty incidents (terrorist attacks, chemical leaks, viral outbreaks), and others can all be anticipated and, to a certain extent, obviated.

Prevention is ideal, but when disaster strikes, the goal is preparedness. With competent consideration, those in charge will not be caught off guard. Though each situation is unique, and none exactly mirrors a practiced scenario, the plans will be in place, and those who implement them will understand their roles.

Initiation is the timing and manner in which a state of emergency is declared. Once declared, the executive must ensure that the entire citizenry is promptly informed of its commencement, termination, purpose, and procedures. The government must go to great lengths to promulgate this information. An individual ought to bear no material burden of discovery nor be subjected to maltreatment, amercement, nor other punitive actions for his or her ignorance of the state of emergency.

Some situations can be expected, such as those due to a slowly moving hurricane; however, other emergencies—perhaps most—cannot be precisely predicted and, consequently, states of emergency cannot be scheduled for a future date. The citizenry should challenge such anticipated states of emergency and search for ulterior motives of those who propose them. In the same vein, states of emergency must never be preventive because preventing an emergency does not, itself, constitute an emergency. Such falls to the purview of the consideration phase.

Implementation is the putting-into-action of whatever plans are in place. Based on what happens in this phase, a crisis is either mitigated or exacerbated. Leadership must be available, decisive, and expedient. Decisions should be actionable, specific, and solution-oriented. Policies implemented during the state of emergency must be designed for discontinuation post termination. Additionally, failure to abide by emergency policies should never be criminalized or otherwise subject to punishment.

A word of caution about states of emergency: Widespread distress, concern, and fear, combined with reduced rights, potentially unreliable information, and increased executive authority swirl together to create a perfect storm of abuse. Possibly the most famous example is Adolf Hitler's *legal* rise to consolidated power—and eventual dictatorship—during the state of emergency that followed the Reichstag fire—an attack on Germany's parliament in 1933. Because history is replete with such examples, the citizenry should be *extremely* wary of leaders who advocate prolonging states of emergency, and request additional authority beyond what has been previously outlined.

Prolongation occurs when a state of emergency has been extended beyond its planned termination. It is the most critical phase; it is also the only discretional one. Prolongation is critical because it is an insidious gateway toward tyranny. It has been proverbial said by many that "power corrupts, and absolute power corrupts absolutely." In a state of emergency, the executive has power that approaches an absolute level.

Prolongation is seldom, if ever, necessary. As stated previously, emergencies are, definitionally, quick. After hours, and certainly not beyond days, the emergent aspect of an emergency wears away, and that which remains is a situation that must be handled in stride. Communities can only be shut down for one day—two at most—but after that, people need society's infrastructure to accomplish their basic necessities. If roads have been blocked, they either need to be cleared or detoured. If grocery stores have been closed, they need to be opened. If emergency services have been diverted, they need to be restored.

Termination is the moment when emergency powers have been revoked from the executive and rights have been restored to the people. This should happen as soon as it is feasible. If smoke has started to fade, then termination should be fast approaching. When substantial portions of the population begin to disobey the emergency procedures, then termination has surely come too late. If people feel comfortable leaving their shelters or participating in non-critical pastimes, then either the state of emergency should have been terminated already, or it should have never been declared in the first place.

As states of emergency are instituted for the citizenry, it has the duty to protect itself from the executive, beginning with peaceful noncompliance. If resistance is encountered, then the executive is immediately suspected of corrupt motives, and the free society must take all appropriate actions to protect its existence and safeguard against totalitarianism.

Checks and balances

States of emergency are delicate balances of cooperation and resistance. The government, its many components, the citizenry, and all others must unite to work through the emergency; at the same time, however, the government must be vigorously subjected to both internal and external checks and balances. Therefore, the following is proposed for each phase:

For consideration: Emergency plans should be drafted by few but approved by many. A plebiscite—that is, a vote cast directly by the people—with at least two-thirds approval of allowances is warranted to decide the limits of the executive's power during a state of emergency. The people must be sober and cautious when granting emergency powers, heeding Benjamin Franklin's timeless warning that "those who would give up essential Liberty, to purchase a little temporary Safety, deserve neither Liberty nor Safety."

For initiation: Declaring a state of emergency is a privilege of the executive; however, a coequal legislature can also declare a state of emergency if there has been a three-fourths vote to do so. A state of emergency cannot be declared sooner than twenty-four hours before it goes into effect. Furthermore, if the commencement of a state of emergency has been declared, its termination needs to have been declared also. It must terminate within forty-eight hours of commencement.

For implementation: The limits of power that had been previously outlined must be adhered to. If the executive or an effector of executive policy, such as a law enforcement or military, breaches the limits that have been established, those offenders must be deposed and replaced with honest persons.

For prolongation: Prolongation can only occur if the executive requests it. Coequal legislature grants approval via a three-fourths vote. To prevent abuse of this concessionary allowance, the vote cannot occur sooner than six hours before the termination, and the extension cannot be more than twenty-four hours from the current termination.

For termination: A state of emergency is terminated under the following circumstances:

1. When the termination datetime has been reached.

2. When the executive declares it.

3. When the coequal legislature calls for it with a majority vote.

4. When the next-highest executive declares it. If a mayor, for example, declares a state of emergency for a city, the governor of the state may terminate it.

5. When the next-highest legislature calls for it with a majority vote.

6. When a majority of the next-lowest level of government—represented by either executives or majority-vote legislatures—call for it.

When it comes to checks and balances, because states of emergency are frequently combined with limitations of rights, and because they are always subject to abuse, prolongation should be difficult, but termination should be easy.

Permissible vs. verboten orders

It should be evident that any powers denied to the government during states of emergency must be always disallowed, and that expressly safeguarded liberties ought to be protected and enshrined in the most fundamental principles of the nation and each polity therein. States of emergencies are designed to handle extraordinary situations and are not free-for-all abuses of power. Therefore, although some rights must necessarily be *temporarily* abridged, most liberties need to be safeguarded from violation. The following is an unordered, inexhaustive list of what allowances the government has though need not always employ, and what liberties are expressly protected in all circumstances.

Allowances. The government may:	Safeguarded liberties. The government may not:
Abridge public means of travel (such as airplanes, cruise ships, trains, and buses)	Abridge private means of travel
Prohibit non-citizens from entering the country	Prohibit citizens from traveling or crossing borders
Seize commercial property	Seize, brutalize, destroy, or vitiate private property
Advise evacuations	Force evacuations or shut off utilities for that purpose
Advise against gatherings	Prohibit gatherings
Recommend curfews	Mandate or enforce curfews
Limit large public activities such as festivals	Limit private activities such as fellowship, parties, and religious functions
Activate the military or its reserves	Conscript or compel civilians into military service
Mandate identification	Mandate travel documents, medical records, proof of activity, or other articles
Advise certain clothing or equipment	Mandate certain clothing or equipment
Recommend content such as radio broadcasts or emergency messaging	Force consumption of such content
Request quartering others in private domiciles	Mandate quartering others in private domiciles

PART 4

EPILOGUE

UNIFICATION

> *The creation of any sense of unity among a population of potentially disharmonious settlers almost always requires the deliberate agency of man. Community is seldom an organic thing, especially among migrants. It needs to be nurtured, facilitated, encouraged.*
>
> ~Simon Winchester, from *The Men Who United the States*

> *You see, we don't need to be the same; our beauty is in the differences. We don't need to agree on everything, but we must work on our listening and learn how to use our self-expression when jamming with others in order to create a better harmony ... We just need to want it. We need to make an effort. So ask yourself: What can you do to bring more harmony to the world?*
>
> ~Miri Ben-Ari

Differences and commonalities

The United States, and more broadly the world, can find strength in its eclecticism. There is a rich panoply of cultures, customs, experiences, and viewpoints that, as a collective, offers more wisdom than can any single component. Among diverse groups, each can learn from the others and benefit greatly. But since these sentiments are widely shared, are they even worth mentioning?

Despite extremely strong emphases on diversity and its

benefits, there is abounding antipathy between every conceivable partition of origin, education, race, religion, gender, age, etc. Sordid scheming and malicious manipulation account for part of this hostility, as some political strategies are designed to profit from division, bitterness, and perceived victimization. However, even choosing to, instead, view humanity in a positive light, there remains an *over*emphasis on differences. Accordingly, we have forgotten to value commonalities.

Before we can gather at the table and consider the viewpoints of those who differ, we must first find the things that bring us together. In a circumstance where heritage, mores, religion, and even preferences of food are different, we must look to whatever brings us to that common circumstance. Do we work for the same employer? Perhaps we can swap stories about what brought us into this field. Do we live in the same locality? In that case, we can confabulate about the traditions that drew us in, or the landscape, or the values. There must be at least some small things that can be celebrated together. It can be holidays, sports, heroes, food, or even sentiments about the weather.

Once we've spent a few minutes engaged with one another—had a conversation, a drink, a musical jam session, a friendly competition, or whatever together—then we can view each other as fellow humans instead of *others*. Chances are that we will even realize that other people are no more evil than we consider ourselves to be. Feeling that way, we safely assume that they have wholesome motivations until there is evidence otherwise. With such sentiments, even if we don't agree, we can at least cooperate to *consider* solutions. We can avoid spite; we can work together where the opportunities are right instead of seeking velitation for nothing more than the sake of conflict.

Barriers and solutions

The world has taken great strides toward equality, and while we are still far from the goal, we should acknowledge and value how much has changed in a relatively brief time. Nevertheless, outstanding problems ought to be identified and addressed, but we must be cautious to avoid drawing erroneous conclusions or seeking redresses that further exacerbate the issues. Namely, there are four great concerns to this end:

1. **Avoid targeting the wrong people.** It is telling that when group A feels marginalized by group B, group B likewise feels at the mercy of group A. As a concrete example, consider the phenomenon in which, on a form or survey—say, hospital admission paperwork—Hispanic people frequently claim to be non-Hispanic, believing that Hispanics will be treated worse, denied benefits, or otherwise negatively targeted, while non-Hispanic people often do just the opposite, claiming that they *are* Hispanic in the belief that Hispanics get reduced pricing, extra benefits, or preferential treatment.

    In cases like these, it stands to reason that neither group fares much better than the other, nor that members of one or the other are party to specific plotting against the other. Even if certain members of those groups secretly scheme against the other, those agents represent a small, independent fraction separate from the larger demographic whole. More likely, though, there is a third party that has—whether intentionally or not—created the circumstances that cause each group to view the other with skepticism and mistrust.

    For the sake of unification, our duty is to reject feelings of misgivings and assume that other groups are not *out to get us* unless there is incontrovertible evidence to that conclusion. We must have the courage and fortitude to avoid taking bad experiences with one person and imputing those feelings to others. It is akin to hating all people with a certain name because, at one point, you met someone with that name who was very disagreeable.

2. **Avoid leaders who focus on differences.** There are some people who champion diversity above all else and sanctimoniously pontificate the same. Policies to this end inhibit the natural process of unification that arises through sharing common spaces and working toward common goals. Furthermore, what they mean by *diversity* is limited, usually to a narrow subset of politically expedient or otherwise demagogic external identifiers such as skin color, language, or gender. There is little appreciation for diversity of experience, attitude, personality, thought process, or anything else that is not visually stunning. These qualities, it is assumed, are captured by a person's external appearance—that all White or Black or bilingual people are, because of those qualities, inherently the same as all their peers. And yet, in truth, two people of opposite color can be exceptionally similar while two people of the same color can be quite different.

Leaders who focus on differences tend to care only about *certain* differences. They will not advocate for all foreigners nor all religions but only some, nor will they be the paladin of short people and world travelers. There simply are not enough five-foot-tall mundivagants to create a strong power base; therefore, *their* diversity is neither particularly welcomed nor valued.

For the sake of unification, our duty is to reject leaders who focus on differences. We need to dismiss people who assert that every form and survey, slice and sliver of information must capture race, gender, and the other demographics about which we are constantly queried. This unceasing corralling sharpens divides and creates mistrust.

3. **Avoid solutions that are fixated on immutable demographics.** Upon identifying an imbalance between demographic groups—race, age, gender, economic status, etc.— the first desire is to correct it at the point-of-notice. For example, if it is discovered and verified that a statistically significant discrepancy exists between the number of blue- and green-eyed people who are employed by publicly-traded companies—that blues are hired in greater numbers than greens—then we, naturally, want to correct whatever is causing this problem.

First, we have a duty to validate this finding and remove any obfuscating differences such as experience, education, geography, or any other factors that might affect the types of people working for which types of companies. From here, there are two possibilities:

Possibility One: The best available evidence strongly indicates that the only discrepancy between blues and greens is indeed their eye color. It seems that a widespread prejudice exists. The incorrect solution is to punish criminally and socially those who employ disproportionate amounts of blue-eyed people, force them to hire more green-eyed people, and consequently cause resentment between all blues and greens. A more favorable solution disallows companies to ask about eye color, and perhaps even has interviewees wear sunglasses to remove that variable and ensure that the best person for each role—regardless of eye color—is hired. If the issue persists, then it falls to the second possibility.

Possibility Two: A disparity between the employment of green- and blue-eyed people does indeed exist, but the root cause is not the eye color itself, but another factor—perhaps experience, as more-experienced people are preferentially hired. It turns out that greens, on average, have less experience than blues. The lack of experience is due to lack of education, and the lack of education is due to lower incomes among the average green-eyed family. A prejudice might have existed at one point in time, perhaps even within living memory, but it is no longer prevalent enough to cause the disparity described. What we are seeing is not due to contemporary bigotry, but due to the effects of a former one.

From here, we, as a society, have a dilemma. Do we address the residual effects of a problem whose solution itself has already been addressed? Suppose that we do. We indeed want to see more green-eyed people in the workplace. What to do now?

First, we reject the superficial, specious approach of requiring companies to hire certain quotas or proportions of greens. We also judiciously withdraw our support and patronage from companies, institutions, universities, etc. that loudly proclaim the copious quantities of greens, browns, grays, and heterochromes comprising their membership. These places have not helped the cause of equality but have hurt it. These policies create avoidance of the majority demographic rather than embrace of the minority ones. They incubate hostility and mistrust, which are quite the opposite of what we really want. A laceration was slowly but surely mending, but they ripped it deeper and stitched only the most superficial layer. The wound looks healthier, but it is worse, and if left unproperly treated, necrosis will set in and effect a crisis.

Instead, we will be prudent and address the heart of the issue. Perhaps at one point the root cause was a ubiquitous prejudice against green-eyed people, but now it is poverty and all its concomitant blights. Again, we must avoid the superficial solution of giving funding or scholarships specific to green-eyed people. This also fosters resentment between blue and greens.

Rather, because the issue is not green-eyedness, per se, but the low incomes experienced by large numbers of these people, we can reason that rendering aid to low-income individuals should encompass the solution. Does this mean that some wealthy greens will miss out on aid while some impoverished blues will receive it? And also, some brown-eyed people about whom we don't have any reliable employment data? Yes, to all three. But here is what we will achieve: Green-eyed people are given a boost to overcome the wrongs of the past, yet, since the solution was not focused on eye color, there is less of a chance that the succor will create a rift between demographics, and there is also less of a chance that the intended correction will *over*correct and pendulum us into a never-ending cycle of wrongs.

Focusing on race, gender, or other immutable demographics—not surprisingly—*focuses* on those particulars. With such an approach, when will it be appropriate to remove the focus and act like we are all equal? Targeting these factors leads to more grouping, more metrics, more oversight, more impositions, and—devastatingly—more division. However, prioritization of geography, poverty, education, and other fluid, non-inherent qualities allow us to correct imbalances without inflaming their original causes. People can move in and out of fluid qualities, but they cannot move in and out of immutable ones.

For the sake of unification, our duty is to reject superficial solutions that focus on immutable demographics rather than fluid demographics and their associated experiences. Except for cases in which prejudices are both demonstrable and institutional, we can safely conclude that the experienced disparities are rooted in issues that can be described by fluid metrics instead of immutable demographics. That is, if green-eyed people really are hired less than blue-eyed people, but the reason is due to poverty, then addressing poverty will address the differences in employment.

4. **Avoid denial of multiple truths.** Two things can be true at once. It is possible to value one's own uniqueness while simultaneously taking pride in a larger collective. For example, a Texan can be proud to be a Texan and embrace that identity, but he can also—without denying his "Texan-ness"—be a proud member of the larger citizenry comprising people who are vastly different in many ways, and in which he is a standout-minority.

It is ironic that, despite ubiquitous calls to embrace the diversity of others, there are equally loud and prevalent calls to dig into one's own immutable demographics and defend their essences with a strong offense of insistence, pride, and showiness. We feel that these ideologies are in conflict, however, and so it puts us in conflict, both with ourselves and with each other. We are told to exceedingly value all the attributes we do not possess while also forming our unique identity from the ones we do.

In reality, and for the sake of unification, our duty is to reject the false mutual exclusivity of these attitudes and instead embrace the idea that we can esteem our own individuality, *and* the uniqueness of our immediate group, *and* the larger whole of which we are a part. Be pleased by whatever heritage led to your green or blue or whichever-color eyes, but do not arrive at the point of valuing your eye color above all else. Take part, and pride, in the larger society that surrounds you.

Unification and conclusion

At the conclusion of this work, you, dear reader, might be wondering what ties it all together. Practical advice for a better world, yes, but the unification of this work is the unification of us. Solutions to our problems exist. They are out there, and they have been proposed time and again. Perhaps unexpectedly, then, our problems remain insufficiently addressed, our questions insufficiently answered.

We cannot hope to accomplish much good while we remain divided, and we cannot unite without conscious efforts to that end. There are multiple approaches, but not all of them are advantageous. Some people wish to see every topic in the context of segregation—male verses female, native verses foreigner, pale verses dark, young verses old, open verses closed, halt verses hale. Those who focus on only these dissimilarities deepen divides and pursue a divergent course that will never resolve. They propose suppressing commonalities and highlighting differences. They insist that the contributions of others are valuable *because those other people are different*.

Instead, we can choose to work with human nature. Forcing new foods down people's throats will not lead to enjoyment, even if the foods are healthy and delicious. Rather, add them to the recipes, complement their flavors, pair them well, and wait for people to savor them on their own. They will come around to appreciate, enjoy, and include those foods in their own cooking.

If you sit in a classroom or arrive at a job and find yourself surrounded by disparate people, the situation can overwhelm. Neither training on, nor pontification about, the worth of these strangers will avert the feelings of isolation and the defenses we naturally create. If someone tries to force you to like your peers, then you will only feel more removed, more suspicious, more resentful.

Alternatively, suppose that as you sit there, feeling a bit lonesome, you must work together to rearrange the furniture and decide on a menu for lunch. You and two others pick up the table and reposition it. You note how they move and act just like you. All three grunted at the weight, but all pulled their weight and set it down together. One of them even ensured that your toes were clear before releasing the load. This person is considerate. Your first choices for lunch were entirely incompatible, but then alternatives were proposed until everyone agreed that the sandwich shop one block over would be fantastic. Perhaps no two people ordered the same item, but you all ate from the same restaurant.

As you and these former strangers collaborate together—small tasks at first, then increasingly complex ones—you achieve, lament, swap stories, and share laughs. In short order, these people whose qualities you questioned because of how different they seemed, you now embrace. You look forward to trying each other's choiciest cuisines and engaging in untried recreation. You value your differences—some of which are stark—yet you realize that there are many commonalities.

At one point, you might have sneered at these people because one enjoys obnoxious music while the other dresses oddly, but now you understand who they are. You've listened to your friend's cacophony and even attended a concert together. You still don't like it, but you can appreciate why he might. And, although you would never choose to wear the clothes that she does, you don't really care. If you were to catch anyone mocking your friends because of who they are, then you would immediately rise to their defense, as they would to yours.

For the sake of unification, our duty is to see each other as fellow people with whom we have many things in common. After we feel united, then we can consider our differences and find value in them. We must dismiss leaders who over-focus on differences. We must resist strong, divisive rhetoric even when, at the surface, it claims to promote unity. The effects of the harmful words can be opposite of their sound. They are wolves disguised as sheep.

Swim Strokes: Vignette of a better world

You have been a swimmer since your teenage years, and your stroke is the freestyle. Putting one hand in front of the other, you glide through the water with speed and efficiency. It's what you know, and it feels natural.

Three years ago, you joined a community pool and were thrilled to find other passionate swimmers. You swam together, coached each other, and formed strong friendships. There were six of you who, when space allowed, liked to share three lanes, and put in at least an hour every Tuesday and Saturday. Of course, you were not the only ones at the pool; namely, there were two strong swimmers—frequent attendees—who swam a few lanes down. They preferred the backstroke, a technique you knew but weren't very good at.

Although previously you never had a problem with the backstroke or any other non-freestyle technique, two years ago new owners took over the pool, and they caused you to resent the backstroke and everyone who used it. The new owners wanted to see more variety at their pool. There were, they believed, too many freestylers and not enough other swimmers, particularly backstrokers. New rules were implemented. At any given time, not more than two-thirds of the swimmers could use the same stroke; also, when lanes were shared, at least one swimmer must be a non-freestyler.

There were some days when you and your five companions were the only people at the pool, but if two of you didn't switch from freestyle to something else—backstroke was the insistence of the owners—then all of you were told to go home. Given all the possible ways to swim, it was unnatural, one owner said, for the pool to have only freestylers. When the pool was crowded, new problems surfaced. Making swimmers with different strokes use the same lanes created mayhem. People were bumping into each other, passing and lapping, abiding different common courtesies.

Theoretically, you should have rejoiced seeing backstrokers at the pool, as their presence meant that you and your friends could use freestyle that day. In contrast, backstrokers began to remind you of the new rules and how they had nearly ruined the joy that swimming once brought you. Somewhere along the way, you and your friends had a subconscious switch, after which you detested not only the backstroke but all of the others: breaststroke, butterfly, sidestroke, and even dog paddle. Anything that was not the freestyle became an inconvenience to you and a threat to your own ability to participate. Enough was enough, you quit the pool.

Thankfully, about one year ago, one of your swim mates reached out and invited you to a new pool that your friends had discovered. It had none of the nonsensical rules adopted by that other one. You and your partner found a lane and began freestyling away. When two swimmers entered the neighboring lane and began backstroking, you felt angry. *These people again!* you thought, not fully understanding the source of your bitterness.

This second pool had its own change of ownership shortly thereafter. Its new proprietors also wanted to see more diversity-of-stroke, but they approached it differently. More than just wanting to see assorted styles, they fundamentally believed that all strokes had their own value. To prove their point, the owners created a friendly competition for the swimmers. There were light giveaways of coupons and gear, but no cash or expensive prizes that would have riled the groups too much.

The competition included several events: One considered only raw speed—the freestylers won this; one measured efficiency by taking swimmers' heart rates before and after—a backstroke-lover took the gold; in another, speed *and* silence were the goal—breaststroke won; the butterfly stroke led the way in style; and finally, a combat-sidestroke swimmer proved most able to swim while carrying a load.

After the event, you saw one of your freestyle friends chatting it up with two backstrokers, both of whom placed quite well and one of whom earned two gold medals. You walked over to congratulate them. You told them how you hadn't thought much of the backstroke and, before today, didn't think that it could outdo freestyle. They expressed similar sentiments from the opposite point of view.

Further into the conversation, you learned that these were the same two swimmers from the first pool. They also left for this new one. It wasn't fair, one of them expressed, for the owners to force a different stroke on other swimmers, and it created a lot of unwanted friction and attention.

These days, your preferred stroke is still the old familiar freestyle, but backstroke is fast becoming a second favorite, and you frequently diversify your workouts by incorporating a little of everything. Your friend group has also grown. You and the backstrokers try to attend at common times. Often, two of you choose to share a lane; yet it wasn't difficult to make it work once you actually wanted to be around each other.

As you look around the water, you smile amusedly. You couldn't get along with other swimmers at the first pool; in fact, despite its ostensible variety, different types of swimmers don't get along there, and it's known around town as an unfriendly place to swim. Here, at this new pool, however, you see everything from championship swimmers to novices—people of all abilities and strokes—but you enjoy the eclecticism and have made many new friends. Other styles bring their own strengths and weaknesses, you now realize, and can complement each other. At the end of the day, you all share the pool together, because more than anyone belongs to a particular stroke, you are all swimmers, and that is the truth you hold most dear.

AFTERWORD

> *Sure I am that this day, now, we are the masters of our fate. That the task which has been set us is not above our strength. That its pangs and toils are not beyond our endurance. As long as we have faith in our cause, and an unconquerable willpower, salvation will not be denied us. In the words of the Psalmist: "He shall not be afraid of evil tidings. His heart is fixed, trusting in the Lord."*
>
> ~Winston Churchill

> *We have it in our power to begin the world over again. A situation, similar to the present, hath not happened since the days of Noah until now. The birthday of a new world is at hand, and a race of men, perhaps as numerous as all Europe contains, are to receive their portion of freedom from the events of a few months. The reflection is awful, and in this point of view, how trifling, how ridiculous, do the little paltry cavilings of a few weak or interested men appear, when weighed against the business of a world.*
>
> ~Thomas Paine, from *Common Sense*

THE AVERAGE PERSON lives better than the kings of old, and this is no exaggeration. Even the impecunious have several, if not dozens or more, outfits; grocery stores have inexpensive fruit, spices, and desserts from across the globe; children have toys and are literate; adults have jewelry and workers' rights; travel is relatively affordable; homes are filled with cushioned furniture, decorations, trinkets, and objects of entertainment. Shall we not be grateful, then, that half of humanity lives like royalty? Nevertheless, acknowledging the possibility of betterment does not mean that we fail to recognize the good that presently exists, nor be appreciative of it.

At the same time, the human race is capable of so much more. We can see it in the abundance already managed, in the starry eyes of adolescents, in the dreams of children.

Regrettably, we have fallen short of our capacity. If we fail due to our own inability, then we cannot begrudge. But such is not the case. We fail because we are engirded by insensate injunctions. We are stuck in ruts because powerbrokers tend toward excessive myopia or hyperopia, overrepresenting and shaping the world around narrow causes or pontificating unactionable broad idealism. We forsake collaboration because we defend solutions rather than purposes, entrenching ourselves in one possibility while neglecting to consider any others.

Despite humanity's incredible achievements, the current state is so sad because it can be so great. Every person, at some point, has had a dream to make the world a better place. Instead of continuing down a course that stifles these visions, we should remove all but the most essential barriers and accelerando into a new era of greatness. As this book strives to offer practical advice, let us ask *How do we begin?*

The starting point for a better world is the *electoral process*. For good or ill, politicians control the world. Supposedly, we—the people—control the politicians, but reality maintains that we have frustratingly little say in the process. Whether we transition into using a single transferable vote or some other—better—method, there absolutely must be a final ballot in which several or more groups can offer candidates for high offices. So long as important positions are reluctantly conceded to one of only two unlovable contestants, we can never hope to elect leaders who offer alternative solutions to the issues we face and break away from the molds we so despise.

So far, we have been given two choices, both unpalatable, but there is a buffet just out of reach. The first-past-the-post electoral process has failed us. Therefore, more importantly than other political concerns, we must use the current system to push forward candidates who will change the electoral process in such a way that new candidates will have a chance of winning. Whether red, blue, or tie-dyed, vote for people who pledge to enact this new voting process. Only after its installation can we begin to systematically target other areas, aiming for solutions that do not pit neighbors against each other, but are broadly agreeable.

Once the single transferable vote is in place, the second steppingstone to a better world is *tax reform*. When people currently think about altering taxation, they limit themselves to increasing or decreasing rates, or perhaps appending to the gallimaufry additional complications like credits, deductions, qualifiers, and disqualifiers. But as the chapter "Taxation" discussed, addressing the process is more important than addressing the revenue itself. The hodgepodge of taxation and the industries that have arisen around it need to be gutted, destroyed, and rebuilt anew, streamlined, and manageable. In the presence of a fair and adequate system of taxation, people will feel empowered to achieve, build, create, and—most importantly—dream once again of building a better world.

When we can elect the people we desire, when we can design processes for themselves and not with regard to their tax burdens, and when we believe that we will reap whatever fruits we sow, then all other possibilities draw near. At that point, choose what inspires you, dear reader, and strive to make it happen. You will have both the means to elect leaders who share your vision as well as the individual resources to begin the process. Is it healthcare? Is it property? Is it unification? Is it pathways to citizenship, coming of age, means of governance, consumer rights, marriage and legal concords, states of emergency and inalienable rights, adminicle and charity, justice and jurisprudence?

∼

These pages pointed out a small handful of systems desperate for reformation, but there are many areas yet undiscussed. There was no mention of infrastructure, about the possibility of decentralizing the majority of power production from vast facilities to individual homes, about designing causeways with heavy thoughtfulness toward pedestrians and bicyclists, about eliminating severe dependance on systems without viable analog or *unplugged* contingencies, or about reducing physical waste.

Infringements of basic liberties were scarcely discussed: violations such as censorship, banning books and even words themselves; injunctions against maintaining personal supplies of necessities such as water, fuel and energy, arms and implements of safety or security, medicine and medical supplies; edicts that transgress the rights to travel, seek employment, avail oneself of legal protections, raise one's own children, or even make one's own medical decisions.

There was no mention of entrepreneurship and how excessive regulations, legal concerns, and other non-essentials force small businesses from the marketplace long before their competitors strike a blow. Neither were there mentions of civic identification, or how there are not clear demarcations between residents and non-residents, nor how the lack of banausic identifiers has led to the necessity and misuse of Social Security numbers.

Agriculture was conspicuously absent, as were discussions

about farming, food production, responsible land management, and the quality of life surrounding farmers and other individuals who pursue the same. Education, too, was a no-show; accordingly, there were no arguments for reforming a system that undervalues educators and leaves their students with little to show after nearly two decades of full-time schooling.

In addition to missing big-ticket items, none of the little things were discussed, like the day-to-day items, the pet peeves, the inconveniences, nor the difficulties unique to certain groups and localities.

∼

The challenge we face is to unite around the common goal of reshaping the world into a place where people can pursue their visions of a better world. We must do away with bureaucratic excesses that, when left unchecked, hamstring even young children attempting a front-yard lemonade stand. We must not let personal squabbles, displeasures, or ideologies become ordinances imposed upon others; we must insist that only essential principles become law. We must streamline the institutions and regulations that are worth retaining; we must design them to be fair, accessible, and dependable; we must strongly question politicians and other power-hungry people who fight for the opposite.

When we grant authority, we must consider that our rivals might one day possess it; therefore, we ought not give free rein to a government run by our preferred leaders, because soon someone else's preference will hold that same power. When we take up a cause, we must consider both our end goal and its concomitant unintended consequences; we must fix our gaze to that goal rather than a particular method of achieving it. When we encounter people of opposing views, we must think of them as people, not villains, and we must consider their reasoning before dismissing, or adopting, their conclusions.

The hope of this book is that you have found its content reasonable, regardless of your background or prior opinions. The hope is that you realized a new way of viewing issues, that you have broken away from one- and two-dimensional solutions, instead emerging into the hitherto unseen spaces of higher dimensions and new perspectives. The hope is that both you, and your archenemy across the political spectrum, can agree that fundamental changes are necessary.

At the outset of this work, I posited that everyone, at some point, has had a vision for a better world, but that nearly all of those dreams were killed by useless impositions. More than anything, the hope of this book is that your dreams have been resurrected and revitalized, and that they will motivate you to stand up, push back, and help instantiate new systems that allow you, and many others, to pursue those dreams and help create a new status quo, an invigorated society, a place of progress, a wholesome—better—world.

> *Let us all unite! Look up! Look up! The clouds are lifting, the sun breaking through. We are coming out of the darkness and into the light. We are coming into a new world: a kind of new world where men will rise above their hate and brutality. The soul of man has been given wings, and at last he is beginning to fly. He is flying into the rainbow, into the light of hope, into the future: that glorious future that belongs to you, to me, and to all of us. Look up. Look up!*
>
> ~Charlie Chaplin, from *The Great Dictator*

ACKNOWLEDGMENTS

MY FANTASTIC WIFE deserves abundant praise and acknowledgment for her unfailing support of my efforts to produce this book. Her reality checks, quality assurance, and indefatigable patience are the reasons these pages made it to the publisher publisher and into your hands.

TO VISIT THE AUTHOR'S WEBSITE,
PLEASE SCAN THE QR CODE BELOW
OR VISIT BENLEBOUTILLIER.COM

www.ingramcontent.com/pod-product-compliance
Lightning Source LLC
LaVergne TN
LVHW041928070526
838199LV00051BA/2744